Communications in Computer and Information Science 2227

Editorial Board Members

Joaquim Filipe ⓘ, *Polytechnic Institute of Setúbal, Setúbal, Portugal*
Ashish Ghosh ⓘ, *Indian Statistical Institute, Kolkata, India*
Lizhu Zhou, *Tsinghua University, Beijing, China*

Rationale

The CCIS series is devoted to the publication of proceedings of computer science conferences. Its aim is to efficiently disseminate original research results in informatics in printed and electronic form. While the focus is on publication of peer-reviewed full papers presenting mature work, inclusion of reviewed short papers reporting on work in progress is welcome, too. Besides globally relevant meetings with internationally representative program committees guaranteeing a strict peer-reviewing and paper selection process, conferences run by societies or of high regional or national relevance are also considered for publication.

Topics

The topical scope of CCIS spans the entire spectrum of informatics ranging from foundational topics in the theory of computing to information and communications science and technology and a broad variety of interdisciplinary application fields.

Information for Volume Editors and Authors

Publication in CCIS is free of charge. No royalties are paid, however, we offer registered conference participants temporary free access to the online version of the conference proceedings on SpringerLink (http://link.springer.com) by means of an http referrer from the conference website and/or a number of complimentary printed copies, as specified in the official acceptance email of the event.

CCIS proceedings can be published in time for distribution at conferences or as post-proceedings, and delivered in the form of printed books and/or electronically as USBs and/or e-content licenses for accessing proceedings at SpringerLink. Furthermore, CCIS proceedings are included in the CCIS electronic book series hosted in the SpringerLink digital library at http://link.springer.com/bookseries/7899. Conferences publishing in CCIS are allowed to use Online Conference Service (OCS) for managing the whole proceedings lifecycle (from submission and reviewing to preparing for publication) free of charge.

Publication process

The language of publication is exclusively English. Authors publishing in CCIS have to sign the Springer CCIS copyright transfer form, however, they are free to use their material published in CCIS for substantially changed, more elaborate subsequent publications elsewhere. For the preparation of the camera-ready papers/files, authors have to strictly adhere to the Springer CCIS Authors' Instructions and are strongly encouraged to use the CCIS LaTeX style files or templates.

Abstracting/Indexing

CCIS is abstracted/indexed in DBLP, Google Scholar, EI-Compendex, Mathematical Reviews, SCImago, Scopus. CCIS volumes are also submitted for the inclusion in ISI Proceedings.

How to start

To start the evaluation of your proposal for inclusion in the CCIS series, please send an e-mail to ccis@springer.com.

Alejandro Bellogin · Ludovico Boratto ·
Styliani Kleanthous · Elisabeth Lex ·
Francesca Maridina Malloci · Mirko Marras
Editors

Advances in Bias and Fairness in Information Retrieval

5th International Workshop, BIAS 2024
Washington, DC, USA, July 18, 2024
Revised Selected Papers

Editors
Alejandro Bellogin
Universidad Autónoma de Madrid
Madrid, Spain

Ludovico Boratto
University of Cagliari
Cagliari, Italy

Styliani Kleanthous
Open University of Cyprus
Nicosia, Cyprus

Elisabeth Lex
Graz University of Technology
Graz, Austria

Francesca Maridina Malloci
University of Cagliari
Cagliari, Italy

Mirko Marras
University of Cagliari
Cagliari, Italy

ISSN 1865-0929 ISSN 1865-0937 (electronic)
Communications in Computer and Information Science
ISBN 978-3-031-71974-5 ISBN 978-3-031-71975-2 (eBook)
https://doi.org/10.1007/978-3-031-71975-2

© The Editor(s) (if applicable) and The Author(s), under exclusive license to Springer Nature Switzerland AG 2025

This work is subject to copyright. All rights are solely and exclusively licensed by the Publisher, whether the whole or part of the material is concerned, specifically the rights of translation, reprinting, reuse of illustrations, recitation, broadcasting, reproduction on microfilms or in any other physical way, and transmission or information storage and retrieval, electronic adaptation, computer software, or by similar or dissimilar methodology now known or hereafter developed.
The use of general descriptive names, registered names, trademarks, service marks, etc. in this publication does not imply, even in the absence of a specific statement, that such names are exempt from the relevant protective laws and regulations and therefore free for general use.
The publisher, the authors and the editors are safe to assume that the advice and information in this book are believed to be true and accurate at the date of publication. Neither the publisher nor the authors or the editors give a warranty, expressed or implied, with respect to the material contained herein or for any errors or omissions that may have been made. The publisher remains neutral with regard to jurisdictional claims in published maps and institutional affiliations.

This Springer imprint is published by the registered company Springer Nature Switzerland AG
The registered company address is: Gewerbestrasse 11, 6330 Cham, Switzerland

If disposing of this product, please recycle the paper.

Advances in Bias and Fairness in Information Retrieval: Preface

The Fifth International Workshop on Algorithmic Bias in Search and Recommendation (BIAS 2024) was held as part of the 47th International ACM SIGIR Conference on Research and Development in Information Retrieval (SIGIR 2024) on July 18, 2024. BIAS 2024 was held in Washington D.C., USA. The workshop was jointly organized by Universidad Autónoma de Madrid (Spain), University of Cagliari (Italy), Open University of Cyprus (Cyprus), and Graz University of Technology (Austria). It was supported by the ACM Conference on Fairness, Accountability, and Transparency (ACM FAccT) Network.

This year, the workshop counted 20 submissions from different countries. All submissions were double-blind peer-reviewed by at least three internal Program Committee members, ensuring that only high-quality work was then included in the final workshop program. The pool of reviewers was strengthened this year, integrating and catching up with both new and accomplished researchers in the field from industry and academia. The final program included 7 full papers.

The workshop day featured engaging paper presentations and a final discussion to highlight open issues and research challenges, and summarize the workshop's outcomes. The accepted contributions were grouped into three thematic sessions, each focusing on distinct aspects of bias and fairness in information retrieval. The first session explored the nature and impact of persuasive techniques in recommendations. The second session covered retention-induced biases in systems with heterogeneous users, the political bias of large language models in few-shot news summarization, and a fairness analysis of machine learning-based code reviewer recommendations. The final session addressed bias reduction techniques, including using agent-based simulations to reduce bias in social networks, mitigating gender bias in neural team recommendations, and the simultaneous unlearning of multiple protected user attributes from variational autoencoder recommenders using adversarial training. More than 30 attendees participated.

In addition to the paper presentations, the program featured two keynote talks. Bhaskar Mitra from Microsoft Research (Canada) delivered the first keynote, titled "Bias and Beyond: On Generative AI and the Future of Search and Society". He emphasized the need for the IR community to address the sociotechnical implications of generative AI, advocating for a proactive research agenda centered on societal needs and integrating fairness, accountability, transparency, and ethics. The second keynote, titled "Bias, Belonging, and the Long-Term Dynamics of Recommender Systems" was given by Nil-Jana Akpinar from Amazon Web Services (USA). She explored the ethical challenges of recommender systems, highlighting the gap between fairness metrics and intuitive notions of equity, and discussed the long-term amplification of biases, as well as the broader impacts on authenticity and exclusion in social networks.

This workshop continued to build on the success of previous editions, with increasing levels of engagement. BIAS 2024 further solidified the community's focus on algorithmic bias and fairness in information retrieval, serving as a crucial forum for discussing ideas and solutions to current challenges. This success inspires us to organize the sixth edition of the workshop next year. We extend our gratitude to the authors and reviewers for helping shape an engaging program, and to the attendees for their active participation.

July 2024

Alejandro Bellogin
Ludovico Boratto
Styliani Kleanthous
Elisabeth Lex
Francesca Maridina Malloci
Mirko Marras

Organization

Workshop Chairs

Alejandro Bellogin — Universidad Autónoma de Madrid, Spain
Ludovico Boratto — University of Cagliari, Italy
Styliani Kleanthous — Open University of Cyprus, Cyprus
Elisabeth Lex — Graz University of Technology, Austria
Francesca M. Malloci — University of Cagliari, Italy
Mirko Marras — University of Cagliari, Italy

Program Committee

Ash Ashokan — University of Nebraska Omaha, USA
Giacomo Balloccu — University of Cagliari, Italy
Timo Breuer — TH Köln, Germany
Iván Cantador — Universidad Autónoma de Madrid, Spain
James Caverlee — Texas A&M University, USA
Yashar Deldjoo — Polytechnic University of Bari, Italy
Giorgio Maria Di Nunzio — University of Padua, Italy
Hossein Fani — University of Windsor, Canada
Saeed Farzi — K. N. Toosi University of Technology, Iran
Alireza Gharahighehi — ITEC - KU Leuven, Belgium
Fabian Haak — TH Köln, Germany
Toshihiro Kamishima — Independent, Japan
Aonghus Lawlor — University College Dublin, Ireland
Cataldo Musto — University of Bari Aldo Moro, Italy
Marinella Petrocchi — IIT-CNR, Italy
Erasmo Purificato — Otto von Guericke Univ. Magdeburg, Germany
Dimitris Sacharidis — Université Libre de Bruxelles, Belgium
Philipp Schaer — TH Köln, Germany
Manel Slokom — Delft University of Technology, The Netherlands
Damiano Spina — RMIT University, Australia
Gian Antonio Susto — University of Padua, Italy
Marko Tkalcic — University of Primorska, Slovenia
Antonela Tommasel — ISISTAN CONICET-UNCPBA, Argentina
Helma Torkamaan — Delft University of Technology, The Netherlands
João Vinagre — Joint Research Centre Eu. Commission, Italy

Emine Yilmaz   Amazon, UK
Eva Zangerle   University of Innsbruck, Austria

Chairs and program committee members are in alphabetical order by last name.

Contents

An Offer You Cannot Refuse? Trends in the Coercive Impact of Amazon
Book Recommendations 1
   Jonathan H. Rystrøm

Retention Induced Biases in a Recommendation System
with Heterogeneous Users 16
   Shichao Ma

Political Bias of Large Language Models in Few-Shot News Summarization ... 32
   Takeshi Onishi and James Caverlee

Fairness Analysis of Machine Learning-Based Code Reviewer
Recommendation 46
   *Mohammad Mahdi Mohajer, Alvine Boaye Belle, Nima Shiri Harzevili,
   Junjie Wang, Hadi Hemmati, Song Wang, and Zhen Ming (Jack) Jiang*

Bias Reduction in Social Networks Through Agent-Based Simulations 64
   Nathan Bartley, Keith Burghardt, and Kristina Lerman

viva*F*emme: Mitigating Gender Bias in Neural Team
Recommendation via Female-Advocate Loss Regularization 78
   *Roonak Moasses, Delaram Rajaei, Hamed Loghmani, Mahdis Saeedi,
   and Hossein Fani*

Simultaneous Unlearning of Multiple Protected User Attributes From
Variational Autoencoder Recommenders Using Adversarial Training 91
   *Gustavo Escobedo, Christian Ganhör, Stefan Brandl, Mirjam Augstein,
   and Markus Schedl*

Author Index 103

An Offer You Cannot Refuse? Trends in the Coercive Impact of Amazon Book Recommendations

Jonathan H. Rystrøm[✉][iD]

Oxford Internet Institute, University of Oxford, Oxford, OX1, UK
jonathan.rystrom@oii.ox.ac.uk

Abstract. Recommender systems can be a helpful tool for recommending content but they can also influence users' preferences. One sociological theory for this influence is that companies are incentivised to influence preferences to make users easier to predict and thus more profitable by making it harder to change preferences. This paper seeks to test that theory empirically. We use *Barrier-to-Exit*, a metric for how difficult it is for users to change preferences, to analyse a large dataset of Amazon Book Ratings from 1998 to 2023. We focus the analysis on users who have changed preferences according to Barrier-to-Exit. To assess the growth of Barrier-to-Exit over time, we developed a linear mixed-effects model with crossed random effects for users and categories. Our findings indicate a highly significant growth of Barrier-to-Exit over time, suggesting that it has become more difficult for the analysed subset of users to change their preferences. However, it should be noted that these findings come with several statistical and methodological caveats including sample bias and construct validity issues related to Barrier-to-Exit. We discuss the strengths and limitations of our approach and its implications. Additionally, we highlight the challenges of creating context-sensitive and generalisable measures for complex socio-technical concepts such as "difficulty to change preferences". We conclude with a call for further research: to curb the potential threats of preference manipulation, we need more measures that allow us to compare commercial as well as non-commercial systems.

Keywords: Recommender Systems · Socio-technical evaluations · Fairness · Search Engines · Audit Study

1 Introduction

What role do recommender systems play in shaping our behaviour? On the one hand, they can seem like a mere convenience: they help us select which music to listen to [26] or which television show to watch [4]. When we provide feedback by liking, rating, buying, or interacting with a product, we hope that our actions help the recommender system "learn" our preferences [20].

However, what if the recommender systems do not simply *learn* our preferences but *shape* them? By providing recommendations, the recommender systems can influence the products we engage with, which can shape our preferences [19]. This creates a feedback loop that can degenerate into so-called filter bubbles and echo chambers [19].

The drivers of this could be commercial. The companies behind the recommender systems might have incentives for shaping our behaviour to increase profitability. This is what Zuboff terms the *prediction imperative* in her exposition of *Surveillance Capitalism* [44]. The prediction imperative states that to secure revenue streams Big Tech companies must become better at predicting the needs of their users. The first step of this is creating better predictive algorithms i.e. going from simple heuristics to sophisticated machine learning [33]. However, as competition increases, the surest way to *predict* behaviour is to *shape* it [44]. By shaping behaviour, companies increase predictability at the cost of the users' autonomy [38].

While it may be good business, changing preferences could plausibly count as manipulation. Apart from harming the autonomy of the users [38], this could have legal implications under the EU AI Act [11,21].

Take the case of Amazon. In 1998, Amazon introduced item-based *collaborative filtering* [24] - a simple and scalable recommender model that allows them to recommend similar items. Since then their models have evolved to create more personalised features using machine learning on sophisticated features [37]. The effects of this have been more accurate recommendations and - crucially - higher sales [40].

The prediction imperative posits that the evolution of Amazon recommender systems should have made it more difficult for users to change preferences to make them more predictable and profitable. They might also steer users towards specific categories that are relatively more profitable [43]. Amazon has hundreds of millions of users. Understanding how these users are affected by the recommender system is important for assessing the societal impacts of large-scale recommendations. Furthermore, such a case study can validate more theoretical claims about biases in recommendation algorithm [1,27]. Similar case study approaches have been used to shed light on, e.g., radicalisation on YouTube [14] and candidate screening algorithms [41].

While a case study of Amazon can yield important insights into the potential coercion of that specific recommender system, the findings cannot necessarily be extended to other recommender systems. As argued by Selbst et al. [36], each system is situated in a specific socio-technical context. A key objective of our paper is to illustrate the process of adapting a measure like Barrier-to-Exit to the context of Amazon's recommender system, highlighting the considerations required for such an adaptation.

To make such a claim it is essential to have methods for empirically analysing potential manipulation. Fortunately, Rakova & Chowdhury [32] provide such a measure: *Barrier-to-Exit*. Barrier-to-Exit provides a measure for how much effort a user must exert to show that they have changed their preferences within a given category. It is built on a theoretical foundation of [36]'s work on fairness traps as well as *systems control theory* as applied to recommender systems [19]. The authors posit that recommender systems with a higher Barrier-to-Exit make it harder to change preferences.

Methods are ineffective without relevant data to apply them to. This may seem insurmountable: Amazon's recommender system is a complex model that builds on a myriad of advanced features including browsing activity, item features, and buying activity [37]. No one but Amazon has access to this data - and they are unlikely to share it [5].

We can get around this to some extent by relying on proxies. Specifically, we can use publicly available ratings as a proxy for user preferences. This has the advantage of being accessible through public datasets [17]. The disadvantage is that we only have access to a (biased) fraction of the data going into the recommender system. In the absence of access to the recommender system, this proxy can indicate the tendencies of coerciveness in the recommender system.

This paper aims to investigate whether Amazon's recommender system has made it more difficult to change preferences over time. To focus the scope, we will only investigate book recommendations, as books were Amazon's first product [37]. This leads us to the following research question:

- **RQ:** Has the Amazon Book Recommender System made it more difficult to change preferences over time?

We take several steps to answer this research question. First, we will formalise Barrier-to-Exit in the context of Amazon book recommendations. We will discuss the caveats of the technique and how it relates to preference change. Then we will use a large dataset of Amazon book recommendations [17] to calculate the Barrier-to-Exit for users who have changed their preferences. We will then analyse the change in Barrier-to-Exit over time using a linear mixed-effects model. Finally, we will discuss the validity and implications of these results.

This paper has two main contributions to the literature: 1) it provides a novel analysis of trends in preference manipulation in a *commercial* rather than *academic* setting. 2) it assesses the portability of Barrier-to-Exit as a measure for real-world datasets.

2 Previous Literature

Several papers have highlighted the need to protect human autonomy and preferences in recommender systems [6,18,38]. However, these focus more on the *normative* need to do so, rather than an *empirical* analysis of the phenomenon. With this paper, we aim to fill this gap in the literature.

Much previous empirical analysis of preference manipulation in recommender systems has focused on the MovieLens-dataset [15]. MovieLens is a movie recommendation platform developed and maintained by the University of Minnesota.[1]

---
[1] movielens.org.

The advantages of this dataset are that it is a) rigorously documented as it is maintained by an academic group; b) freely available; and c) well-structured, thus making analysis easier. However, because it is a non-commercial project it is not susceptible to surveillance capitalistic imperatives to the same extent as e.g. Amazon [44].

Nguyen et al. [30] analysed whether MovieLens users were exposed to less diverse content over time - a type of preference manipulation. While they found a significant (albeit small) decrease, the effect was smaller for users who followed the recommendations than the users who did not. However, as discussed by Rakova & Chowdhury [32], they focus their analysis on highly active and highly nonactive users neglecting the middle. Also, content diversity is an important but incomplete measure of preference manipulation.

Rakova & Chowdhury [32] also use the MovieLens dataset to define and showcase Barrier-to-Exit. However, their paper is more of a proof-of-concept rather than an analysis. The present paper expands on [32] by applying the metric to a real-world dataset of a commercial recommender system.

Similarly, Chaney et al. [8] argue that the feedback loops between users and recommender systems can cause homogenisation of behaviour. These effects can be difficult to control for in evaluations since the evaluation data is shaped by the feedback loops. The feedback loops might give rise to biases in the recommendations. One well-studied bias is *popularity bias* [1,27], where more popular items are recommended more often. Naghiaei et al. [27] note that collaborative filtering algorithms are particularly prone to popularity bias and that diverse and niche users are the most affected. These findings are corroborated by Kowald et al. [22], who find that users disinterested in popular content pay a price in terms of miscalibration and accuracy.

Through the analysis in this paper, we aim to investigate these effects through a real-world case study of the Amazon book recommender system. As argued by Selbst et al. [36] auditing real-world systems allows us to take a *socio-technical* stance that takes into consideration the social context of the system. Much of the previous research cited uses either simulations [16] or focuses on the recommendation algorithms [1,27]. That focus is a key step in uncovering different types of bias - validating the results through case studies can further strengthen the research area.

3 Methods and Data

3.1 Defining Barrier-to-Exit

Barrier-to-Exit quantifies the effort required for users to change their preferences within a recommender system, focusing on how *revealed preferences* for categories change over time relative to interaction thresholds. This concept is illustrated in Fig. 1, adapted from Rakova & Chowdhury [32], showing the user-AI interaction feedback loops.

In this context, the user's interest (μ_t) evolves and is influenced by previously recommended items (α_{t-1}) and user actions (c_t). The Recommender System (Θ_t)

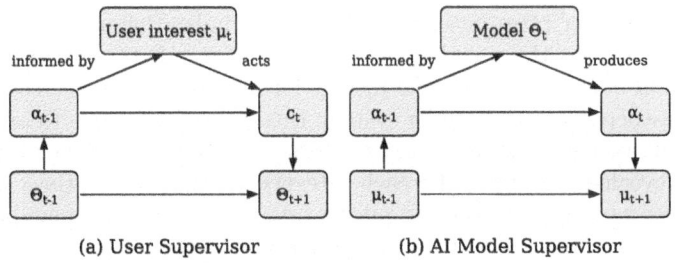

Fig. 1. Control flow in Recommender Systems from user (a) and AI model (b) perspectives. Adapted from [32].

updates based on user feedback and past recommendations, presenting new items (α_t) that shape future interests. Thus, the Recommender System and the user dynamically influence each other based on their interactions.

To calculate Barrier-to-Exit, we measure changes in revealed preferences, c_t^i, which aggregate the ratings r_{tj} weighted by category-relevance m_{tj}^i, across rated books within a category i over time t:

$$c_t^i = \sum_{j=1}^{n} m_{tj}^i \cdot r_{tj} \qquad (1)$$

Category-relevance represents how closely a book fits a category, calculated using an unsupervised approach based on category co-occurrence. Details of the implementation are available on the project's GitHub repository.

Interaction thresholds define the typical range of a user's ratings for a category, adjusted over time using a rolling window. The upper (X_t^i) and lower (Y_t^i) thresholds are calculated as:

$$X_t^i = \text{mean}(c_{t-v}, \ldots, c_t) + 2 \times \text{std}(c_{t-v}, \ldots, c_t) \qquad (2)$$
$$Y_t^i = \text{mean}(c_{t-v}, \ldots, c_t) - 2 \times \text{std}(c_{t-v}, \ldots, c_t) \qquad (3)$$

The thresholds help model the expected user behaviour as perceived by the AI model.

Barrier-to-Exit for a category is then the sum of preferences falling between these thresholds over a period where a change is noted:

$$BarrierToExit_{t_y}^i = \sum_{\tau \in (t_x, t_y)} c_\tau^i \quad \text{such that} \quad Y_\tau < c_\tau^i < X_\tau \qquad (4)$$

This measure applies to users demonstrating a sufficient number of varied ratings in a category, allowing for meaningful analysis of preference shifts.

To illustrate the concept of Barrier-to-Exit, consider a user who initially prefers mystery novels but gradually shifts their interest towards science fiction.

Initially, the user rates mystery novels highly, indicating a strong preference for this category. As the user begins exploring science fiction, their ratings for science fiction books increase while ratings for mystery novels decrease.

In a non-coercive recommender system, this transition is smooth and responsive to the user's changing preferences. The system tracks the user's ratings and calculates revealed preferences for each category. As the user's ratings for science fiction books increase, the system quickly adapts to the user's new preference, resulting in a low Barrier-to-Exit. This makes it easier for the user to change preferences, arguably increasing their self-determination [32].

Conversely, in a coercive recommender system, the transition is slow and resistant to change. Despite the user's increasing ratings for science fiction, the system continues to predominantly recommend mystery novels, maintaining the status quo. This behavior results in a high Barrier-to-Exit, requiring significant effort or time for the user to shift visible preferences. This resistance may lead to frustration as the system clings to outdated preferences.

Thus, a non-coercive recommender system with a lower Barrier-to-Exit allows for a quicker and more seamless transition in user preferences, while a coercive system with a high Barrier-to-Exit hinders this transition.

In this section, we've outlined the core aspects of Barrier-to-Exit, emphasizing its role in measuring the effort required to change user preferences within a category. For further details, including code and implementation nuances, please refer to our GitHub repository.

3.2 Data

Our analysis utilizes the Amazon book reviews dataset, spanning from 1998 to 2023, comprising approximately 51 million ratings from about 15 million users, all on a 1–5 Likert scale [17]. This data is publicly accessible, albeit without a datasheet beyond simple statistics, posing potential limitations on assessing coverage or bias [12].

To align with our focus on preference changes, we filtered for users who have provided more than 20 ratings, mirroring the criteria used in the original definition of Barrier-to-Exit [15,32]. This subset, illustrated in Fig. 2, retains approximately 22% of the ratings but only represents about 1.2% of the users, with a final analytical cohort of 15,122 users who demonstrate preference changes in the period of the study.

We complemented the ratings with category data for each book, filtering for the top most used 500 categories to simplify computation and ensure relevance. The implementation details for processing this category-similarity are available on our GitHub repository.

This approach allows us to focus on users whose behaviour provides insights into the dynamics of preference change within Amazon's recommendation system, although it is restricted to those actively participating through ratings. Further implications of this subset selection are discussed in the later sections.

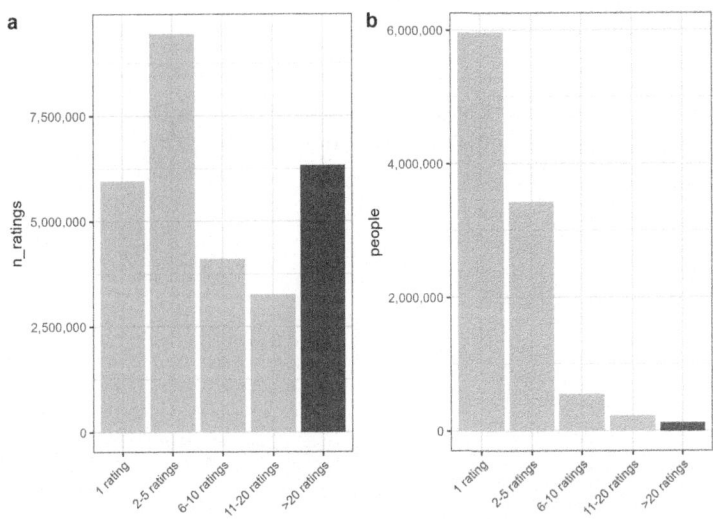

Fig. 2. Distribution of total amount of ratings and people across different rating-activity groups, highlighting the subset with more than 20 ratings.

3.3 Model

To analyse trends in Barrier-to-Exit, we employ a crossed multi-level model that accounts for individual user differences and category-specific characteristics [2,37,44]. This model includes over 300 categories treated as random effects due to their number and variability [25].

The updated model is formalised as:

$$y_{ij} = \beta_0 + \beta_1 X_{1i} + \beta_2 X_{2i} + \beta_3 (X_{1i} \times X_{2i}) + e_i + e_j \qquad (5)$$

where y_{ij} represents the log-transformed Barrier-to-Exit for user i and category j, allowing us to interpret changes exponentially as percentage increases [39]. X_{1i} and X_{2i} indicate time (in quarters since 1998) and user activity level (logged), respectively. The term $(X_{1i} \times X_{2i})$ represents the interaction between time and user activity level, capturing how the effect of time on Barrier-to-Exit changes with different levels of user activity. The terms e_i and e_j represent random errors for the users and categories, respectively, capturing the unobserved heterogeneity at these levels.

The main role of the activity parameters, including the interaction term, is to account for the relationship between activity, Barrier-to-Exit, and time as seen in Fig. 3. Thus, these parameters control for these interactions, allowing us to obtain a cleaner estimate of the increase in Barrier-to-Exit over time. Without controlling for activity, an increase in Barrier-to-Exit might be confounding by the trend in 3b.

Significance testing is conducted using Satterthwaite's approximation [23,35], appropriate given the large sample size, which ensures robustness against Type

I errors [2,13]. The hypothesis tested posits a significant increase in Barrier-to-Exit over time:

- **Hypothesis**: There has been a significant increase in Barrier-to-Exit for the Amazon Book Recommender System from 1998 to 2023.

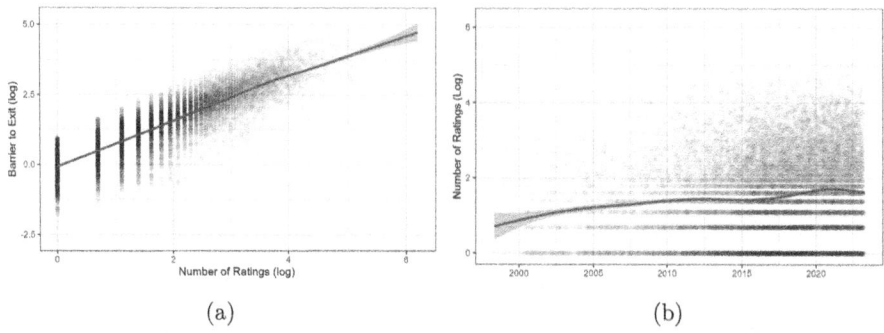

Fig. 3. Plots of the activity level, defined as the number of ratings in the period of Barrier-to-Exit. Fig. 3a: The relation between activity-level and Barrier-to-Exit. Notice the strong linearity. Fig. 3b: Change in activity-level over time. The regression lines are non-parametric GAM regression [42]. Note that while there is no strong relation between activity level and time, there has been a substantial increase in the density of points, reflecting Amazon's increased popularity [40].

Model fit is evaluated using marginal and conditional R^2_{LMM} [3,28], providing insight into the variance explained by fixed and random effects. Figure 3a and 3b visually depict the relation between user activity levels and Barrier-to-Exit, highlighting both the strong linear relationship and the changing activity levels over time.

This model allows us to quantify how user interactions and category features influence the difficulty of changing preferences in Amazon's book recommendation system, with further implications discussed in Sect. 5.2.

4 Results

The results from the model can be seen in Table 1. The coefficient for time is 0.005 (SE=0.001). This implies growth in Barrier-to-Exit of approximately 0.5% per year. This is highly significant (T=6.102, $p \ll 0.0001$). The coefficient for activity level is 0.760 (SE=0.009), which is also highly significant (T=80.199, $p \ll 0.0001$). The interaction term between time and activity level is 0.002 (SE=0.0005), indicating that the effect of time on Barrier-to-Exit increases with higher activity levels, and this interaction is significant (T=3.925, $p = 8.69 \times 10^{-5}$).

Table 1. Main Results

	Dependent variable: Barrier-to-Exit (Log)
Time (years)	0.005*** (0.001)
Activity-level (Log)	0.760*** (0.009)
Time-Activity Interaction	0.002*** (0.0005)
Intercept	0.413*** (0.045)
Unique Users	15,122
Unique Categories	152
Marginal R^2	0.695
Conditional R^2	0.907
Observations	24,604
Note:	*p<0.1; **p<0.05; ***p<0.01

The marginal R^2 is 0.695, indicating that 69.5% of the variance is explained by the fixed effects. The conditional R^2 is 0.907, meaning that 90.7% of the variance is explained by the random and fixed effects combined.

A visual representation of these models can be seen in Fig. 4. The partial effects plot [10] in Fig. 4a shows an increase in Barrier-to-Exit from approximately 1.57 to 1.8. This translates into a growth of approximately 23% throughout the study. Figure 4b shows the effect plot with residuals.

5 Discussion

5.1 Key Findings

Our research aimed to determine whether Amazon's Book Recommender System has made it increasingly difficult for users to change their preferences over time. The analysis demonstrates a significant growth in Barrier-to-Exit, increasing by approximately 23% from 1998 to 2023 (see Fig. 4). As seen in Fig 4b, the trend has quite some variance. Nevertheless, the high statistical significance of the results indicates that they are indeed robust. This growth suggests that the system has become more effective at maintaining user preferences within certain categories, potentially limiting exposure to diverse content and reinforcing existing biases.

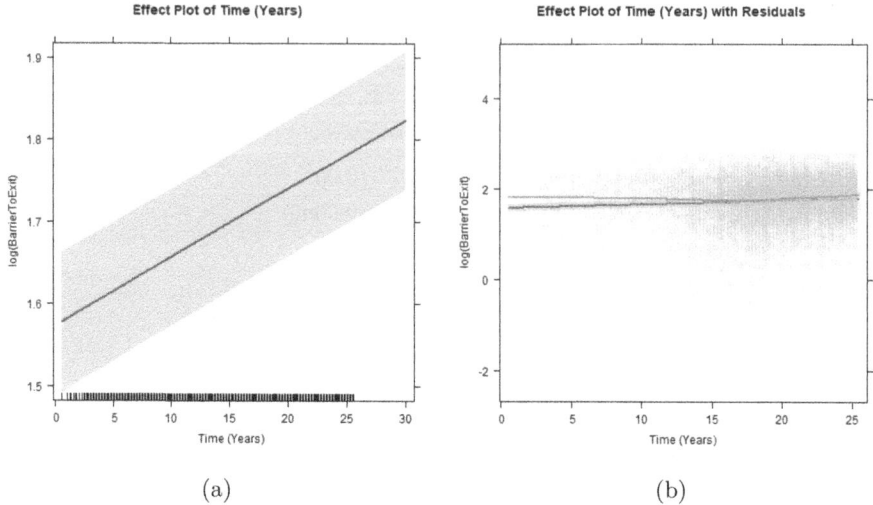

Fig. 4. Effect plots for Year. Fig. 4a shows the partial effect plot. Fig. 4b shows the same but with residuals added. The X-axis shows years after the beginning of the dataset (1998 = 0). The orange line in Fig. 4b is a non-parametric line of best fit.

5.2 Strengths and Limitations

The main strength of our study is its large scale, which provides robust statistical power to detect even small effect sizes associated with changes in Barrier-to-Exit. This allows for a detailed exploration of trends over a substantial period, showcasing the evolving influence of the recommender system. Furthermore, by focusing on the Amazon book recommender system, we can adapt the Barrier-to-Exit metric to its specific context, which makes for a more accurate appraisal of user preferences.

However, significant limitations affect the interpretation of our findings. Primarily, the validity of using ratings as a proxy for user interaction is limited, as it captures only a fraction of user activities on Amazon. Ratings represent explicit feedback, which may not fully encompass the implicit preferences users demonstrate through other interactions such as browsing and purchasing behaviors. Additionally, research shows that ratings tend to be skewed towards extremes, as users are more likely to rate books they feel strongly about resulting in a lack of data on more moderate interactions [9]. These limitations mean we get a less granular view of user preferences and must focus on very active users who provide multiple ratings. Incorporating data on browsing and purchasing behaviours could alleviate these problems by providing a more granular view of user preferences and allowing us to measure the Barrier-to-Exit for a wider range of users. Obtaining such data would likely require collaboration with system providers in an audit-like fashion (see, e.g., [31,34,41]).

5.3 Implications and Further Research

The observed increase in Barrier-to-Exit raises significant concerns regarding user autonomy and the potential for preference manipulation within Amazon's recommendation system. This finding aligns with previous research on filter bubbles and popularity bias [1,30]. Furthermore, the results suggest that the theoretical results about user homogenisation and the pernicious effects of miscalibration [16,22] hold in real-world recommender systems.

The dynamics of preference change and the role of measures like Barrier-to-Exit in auditing recommender systems are critical, particularly in light of new regulations such as the EU AI Act [21]. Future research should address the limitations identified by exploring methods to capture a broader spectrum of user interactions and developing metrics that can be applied across various types of user activities. Including data on browsing and purchasing behaviours, in addition to ratings, would provide a more nuanced understanding of user preferences and how they are shaped by recommender systems. Establishing collaborative studies with platforms that can provide more detailed data could enhance the robustness of such analyses. Additionally, the introduction of 'sock puppet'-auditing [34] and other innovative auditing techniques could provide deeper insights into system-level behaviours and their impacts on user preferences. However, these methods come with their own ethical and practical challenges, which must be carefully managed.

The observed increase in Barrier-to-Exit raises significant concerns regarding user autonomy and the potential for preference manipulation within Amazon's recommendation system. Such manipulation could have implications for consumer choice and fairness, emphasizing the need for recommendation systems that support diverse user experiences and prevent the formation of filter bubbles [29].

While this paper focuses on Amazon, future research could gain valuable insights by studying other platforms. Chinese platforms such as Temu and Shein, in particular, offer interesting case studies because they operate under different Surveillance Capitalism dynamics [7,44]. Future research will need to adapt the Barrier-to-Exit metric, especially regarding user preferences, to fit the context and available data of these platforms.

In conclusion, while our study indicates that Amazon's recommendation algorithms have likely increased the Barrier-to-Exit for users, further work is needed to fully understand the implications of these findings and to develop more inclusive and transparent recommender systems. Future studies should aim to include a wider range of user interactions and to design metrics that not only capture changes in user preferences but also respect user privacy and autonomy. This will be crucial for ensuring that recommender systems enhance user experience without compromising ethical standards.

6 Conclusion

Understanding how recommender systems shape our behaviour is essential to avoid manipulation. In this paper, we investigated the Amazon recommender system concerning whether it has made it harder to change preferences. By analysing the Barrier-to-Exit [32] of more than 15,000 users, we found a highly significant growth in Barrier-to-Exit over time, which indicates that it has indeed become harder to change preferences for the analysed users.

However, sampling bias induced by the calculation of Barrier-to-Exit makes it difficult to draw conclusions about the general population of Amazon customers. This highlights the dilemma of portability in measuring socio-technical systems [36]: accurately evaluating a concept like "changing preferences" requires adapting to the context of the system, which makes it more difficult to generalise (and compare) to other systems.

Comparing recommender systems is necessary for ensuring that these respect human autonomy [38] and live up to new regulations such as the EU AI Act [21]. Future work should aim to create auditing procedures and metrics that allow third parties to measure potential preference manipulation in a way that fits within the context of the industry *and* allows for comparisons between different systems. Expanding the scope of interactions analyzed and developing adaptable metrics will be key steps in assessing the pressures of *Surveillance Capitalism* [44] on human autonomy.

References

1. Abdollahpouri, H., Mansoury, M., Burke, R., Mobasher, B.: The Unfairness of Popularity Bias in Recommendation (Sep 2019). https://doi.org/10.48550/arXiv.1907.13286, http://arxiv.org/abs/1907.13286, arXiv:1907.13286 [cs]
2. Baayen, R.H., Davidson, D.J., Bates, D.M.: Mixed-effects modeling with crossed random effects for subjects and items. J. Mem. Lang. **59**(4), 390–412 (2008). publisher: Elsevier
3. Bartoń, K.: MuMIn: multi-Model Inference (Sep 2022). https://CRAN.R-project.org/package=MuMIn
4. Bennett, J., Lanning, S.: The netflix prize. In: Proceedings of KDD Cup And Workshop, vol. 2007, pp. 35. New York (2007)
5. Burrell, J.: How the machine 'thinks': understanding opacity in machine learning algorithms. Big Data & Society **3**(1), 2053951715622512 (2016). https://doi.org/10.1177/2053951715622512, https://ezproxy-prd.bodleian.ox.ac.uk:2246/doi/full/10.1177/2053951715622512, publisher: SAGE Publications Ltd
6. Calvo, R.A., Peters, D., Vold, K., Ryan, R.M.: Supporting human autonomy in AI Systems: a framework for ethical enquiry. In: Burr, C., Floridi, L. (eds.) Ethics of Digital Well-Being: a Multidisciplinary Approach, pp. 31–54. Philosophical Studies Series, Springer International Publishing, Cham (2020). https://doi.org/10.1007/978-3-030-50585-1_2, https://doi.org/10.1007/978-3-030-50585-1_2

7. Chan, N.K., Kwok, C.: The politics of platform power in surveillance capitalism: a comparative case study of ride-hailing platforms in China and the United States. Glob. Media China **7**(2), 131–150 (2022). https://doi.org/10.1177/20594364211046769, https://doi.org/10.1177/20594364211046769, publisher: SAGE Publications Ltd
8. Chaney, A.J.B., Stewart, B.M., Engelhardt, B.E.: How algorithmic confounding in recommendation systems increases homogeneity and decreases utility. In: Proceedings of the 12th ACM Conference on Recommender Systems, pp. 224–232. RecSys '18, Association for Computing Machinery, New York, NY, USA (Sep 2018). https://doi.org/10.1145/3240323.3240370, https://dl.acm.org/doi/10.1145/3240323.3240370
9. Dalvi, N., Kumar, R., Pang, B.: Para 'Normal' activity: on the distribution of average ratings. In: Proceedings of the International AAAI Conference on Web and Social Media vol. 7, number. 1, pp. 110–119 (2013). https://doi.org/10.1609/icwsm.v7i1.14427, https://ojs.aaai.org/index.php/ICWSM/article/view/14427, number: 1
10. Fox, J.: Effect displays in R for generalised linear models. J. Stat. Softw. **8**(15) (2003). https://doi.org/10.18637/jss.v008.i15, http://www.jstatsoft.org/v08/i15/
11. Franklin, M., Ashton, H., Gorman, R., Armstrong, S.: Missing mechanisms of manipulation in the EU AI Act. In: The International FLAIRS Conference Proceedings, vol. 35 (May 2022). https://doi.org/10.32473/flairs.v35i.130723, https://journals.flvc.org/FLAIRS/article/view/130723
12. Gebru, T., et al.: Datasheets for Datasets (Dec 2021). http://arxiv.org/abs/1803.09010, arXiv:1803.09010 [cs]
13. Ghasemi, A., Zahediasl, S.: Normality tests for statistical analysis: a guide for non-statisticians. Int. J. Endocrinol. Metab.**10**(2), 486–489 (2012). https://doi.org/10.5812/ijem.3505, https://brief.land/ijem/articles/71904.html
14. Haroon, M., Chhabra, A., Liu, X., Mohapatra, P., Shafiq, Z., Wojcieszak, M.: YouTube, The Great Radicalizer? Auditing and Mitigating Ideological Biases in YouTube Recommendations (Mar 2022). http://arxiv.org/abs/2203.10666, arXiv:2203.10666 [cs]
15. Harper, F.M., Konstan, J.A.: The movielens datasets: history and context. ACM Trans. Interact. Intell. Syst. **5**(4), 1–19 (2016). https://doi.org/10.1145/2827872, https://dl.acm.org/doi/10.1145/2827872
16. Harper, F.M., Konstan, J.A.: The MovieLens datasets: history and context. ACM Trans. Interact. Intell. Syst. **5**(4), 1–19 (2016). https://doi.org/10.1145/2827872, https://dl.acm.org/doi/10.1145/2827872
17. Hou, Y., Li, J., He, Z., Yan, A., Chen, X., McAuley, J.: Bridging Language and Items for Retrieval and Recommendation (Mar 2024). http://arxiv.org/abs/2403.03952, arXiv:2403.03952 [cs]
18. Jannach, D., Adomavicius, G.: Recommendations with a Purpose. In: Proceedings of the 10th ACM Conference on Recommender Systems, pp. 7–10. ACM, Boston Massachusetts USA (Sep 2016). https://doi.org/10.1145/2959100.2959186, https://dl.acm.org/doi/10.1145/2959100.2959186
19. Jiang, R., Chiappa, S., Lattimore, T., György, A., Kohli, P.: Degenerate feedback loops in recommender systems. In: Proceedings of the 2019 AAAI/ACM Conference on AI, Ethics, and Society, pp. 383–390. ACM, Honolulu HI USA (Jan 2019). https://doi.org/10.1145/3306618.3314288, https://dl.acm.org/doi/10.1145/3306618.3314288

20. Knijnenburg, B.P., Reijmer, N.J., Willemsen, M.C.: Each to his own: how different users call for different interaction methods in recommender systems. In: Proceedings of the fifth ACM conference on Recommender systems, pp. 141–148. RecSys '11, Association for Computing Machinery, New York, NY, USA (Oct 2011). https://doi.org/10.1145/2043932.2043960, https://doi.org/10.1145/2043932.2043960
21. Kop, M.: EU Artificial Intelligence Act: The European Approach to AI pp. 11 (Nov 2021)
22. Kowald, D., Mayr, G., Schedl, M., Lex, E.: A Study on accuracy, miscalibration, and popularity bias in recommendations. In: Boratto, L., Faralli, S., Marras, M., Stilo, G. (eds.) Advances in Bias and Fairness in Information Retrieval, pp. 1–16. Springer Nature Switzerland, Cham (2023). https://doi.org/10.1007/978-3-031-37249-0_1
23. Kuznetsova, A., Brockhoff, P.B., Christensen, R.H.B.: lmerTest package: tests in linear mixed effects models. J. stat. softw. **82**(13) (2017), publisher: The Foundation for Open Access Statistics
24. Linden, G., Smith, B., York, J.: Amazon. com recommendations: item-to-item collaborative filtering. IEEE Internet comput. **7**(1), 76–80 (2003). publisher: IEEE
25. Maddala, G.S.: The use of variance components models in pooling cross section and time series data. Econometrica **39**(2), 341 (1971). https://doi.org/10.2307/1913349, https://www.jstor.org/stable/1913349?origin=crossref
26. Millecamp, M., Htun, N.N., Jin, Y., Verbert, K.: Controlling spotify recommendations: effects of personal characteristics on music recommender user interfaces. In: Proceedings of the 26th Conference on User Modeling, Adaptation and Personalization, pp. 101–109 (2018)
27. Naghiaei, M., Rahmani, H.A., Dehghan, M.: The unfairness of popularity bias in book recommendation. In: Boratto, L., Faralli, S., Marras, M., Stilo, G. (eds.) Advances in Bias and Fairness in Information Retrieval, pp. 69–81. Springer International Publishing, Cham (2022). https://doi.org/10.1007/978-3-031-09316-6_7
28. Nakagawa, S., Johnson, P.C., Schielzeth, H.: The coefficient of determination R 2 and intra-class correlation coefficient from generalized linear mixed-effects models revisited and expanded. J. Roy. Soc. Interface **14**(134), 20170213 (2017). publisher: The Royal Society
29. Nguyen, C.T.: Echo chambers and epistemic bubbles. Episteme **17**(2), 141–161 (2020). publisher: Cambridge University Press
30. Nguyen, T.T., Hui, P.M., Harper, F.M., Terveen, L., Konstan, J.A.: Exploring the filter bubble: the effect of using recommender systems on content diversity. In: Proceedings of the 23rd International Conference On World Wide Web - WWW '14, pp. 677–686. ACM Press, Seoul, Korea (2014). https://doi.org/10.1145/2566486.2568012, http://dl.acm.org/citation.cfm?doid=2566486.2568012
31. Raji, I.D., et al.: Closing the AI Accountability Gap: Defining an End-to-End Framework for Internal Algorithmic Auditing (Jan 2020). https://doi.org/10.48550/arXiv.2001.00973, http://arxiv.org/abs/2001.00973, arXiv:2001.00973 [cs]
32. Rakova, B., Chowdhury, R.: Human self-determination within algorithmic sociotechnical systems (Sep 2019). http://arxiv.org/abs/1909.06713, arXiv:1909.06713 [cs]
33. Raschka, S., Patterson, J., Nolet, C.: Machine learning in python: main developments and technology trends in data science, machine learning, and artificial intelligence. Information **11**(4), 193 (2020). publisher: Multidisciplinary Digital Publishing Institute

34. Sandvig, C., Hamilton, K., Karahalios, K., Langbort, C.: Auditing algorithms: research methods for detecting discrimination on internet platforms. Data discrimination converting crit. concerns productive inq. **22**, 4349–4357 (2014)
35. Satterthwaite, F.E.: An approximate distribution of estimates of variance components. Biometrics Bull. **2**(6), 110 (1946). https://doi.org/10.2307/3002019, https://www.jstor.org/stable/10.2307/3002019?origin=crossref
36. Selbst, A.D., boyd, d., Friedler, S.A., Venkatasubramanian, S., Vertesi, J.: Fairness and abstraction in sociotechnical systems. In: Proceedings of the Conference on Fairness, Accountability, and Transparency, pp. 59–68. ACM, Atlanta GA USA (Jan 2019). https://doi.org/10.1145/3287560.3287598, https://dl.acm.org/doi/10.1145/3287560.3287598
37. Smith, B., Linden, G.: Two decades of recommender systems at Amazon.com. IEEE Internet Comput. **21**(3), 12–18 (2017). https://doi.org/10.1109/MIC.2017.72, http://ieeexplore.ieee.org/document/7927889/
38. Varshney, L.R.: Respect for Human Autonomy in Recommender Systems (Sep 2020). http://arxiv.org/abs/2009.02603, arXiv:2009.02603 [cs]
39. Villadsen, A.R., Wulff, J.N.: Statistical myths about log-transformed dependent variables and how to better estimate exponential models. Br. J. Manag. **32**(3), 779–796 (2021). https://doi.org/10.1111/1467-8551.12431, https://onlinelibrary.wiley.com/doi/10.1111/1467-8551.12431
40. Wells, J.R., Danskin, G., Ellsworth, G.: Amazon. com, 2018. Harvard Business School Case Study (716-402) (2018)
41. Wilson, C., et al.: Building and auditing fair algorithms: a case study in candidate screening. In: Proceedings of the 2021 ACM Conference on Fairness, Accountability, and Transparency, pp. 666–677. FAccT '21, Association for Computing Machinery, New York, NY, USA (Mar 2021). https://doi.org/10.1145/3442188.3445928, https://doi.org/10.1145/3442188.3445928
42. Wood, S.N., Pya, N., Säfken, B.: Smoothing parameter and model selection for general smooth models. J. Am. Stat. Assoc. **111**(516), 1548–1563 (2016). https://doi.org/10.1080/01621459.2016.1180986, https://doi.org/10.1080/01621459.2016.1180986, publisher: Taylor & Francis _eprint: https://doi.org/10.1080/01621459.2016.1180986
43. Zhu, F., Liu, Q.: Competing with complementors: an empirical look at Amazon.com. Strateg. Manag. J. **39**(10), 2618–2642 (2018). https://doi.org/10.1002/smj.2932, https://onlinelibrary.wiley.com/doi/abs/10.1002/smj.2932, _eprint: https://onlinelibrary.wiley.com/doi/pdf/10.1002/smj.2932
44. Zuboff, S.: The Age of Surveillance Capitalism: The Fight for a Human Future at the New Frontier of Power: Barack Obama's Books of 2019. Profile Books (2019)

Retention Induced Biases in a Recommendation System with Heterogeneous Users

Shichao Ma

Yelp Inc., San Francisco, CA 94105, USA
shichaom@yelp.com

Abstract. I examine a conceptual model of a recommendation system (RS) with user inflow and churn dynamics. When inflow and churn balance out, the user distribution reaches a steady state. Changing the recommendation algorithm alters the steady state and creates a transition period. During this period, the RS behaves differently from its new steady state. In particular, A/B experiment metrics obtained in transition periods are biased indicators of the RS's long-term performance. Scholars and practitioners, however, often conduct A/B tests shortly after introducing new algorithms to validate their effectiveness. This A/B experiment paradigm, widely regarded as the gold standard for assessing RS improvements, may consequently yield false conclusions. I also briefly touch on the data bias caused by the user retention dynamics.

Keywords: Recommendation system · A/B experimentation · Bias · User retention and churn · System convergence

1 Introduction

Running a recommendation system (RS) is rarely a one-shot game. For example, YouTube was founded in 2005 and has been serving users for nearly two decades.[1] In any long running RS, users join and leave over time. To be successful in the long run, it is critical for developers to constantly enhance the RS, attract new users and retain existing ones.

A key improvement of great theoretical value is improving the quality of the recommendation. Throughout this paper, recommendation quality refers to the general attractiveness of the recommended items and the general efficacy of the recommendation algorithm. It represents the core user experience that an RS can offer. Users may lose interest and leave the platform if they find the recommended items irrelevant. Conversely, high recommendation quality may encourage more users to stay, which leads to the long term success of the RS.

However, the mainstream RS literature does not explicitly consider the above dynamics. Most studies assume the user is a fixed set or has a fixed distribution

---

[1] https://en.wikipedia.org/wiki/History_of_YouTube.

and focus on recommendation algorithms that optimize some transient measures of recommendation quality given the fixed user distribution [5–7, 12–15, 19, 23–25, 30, 33].

This literature leaves an important question unanswered: Does an RS that explicitly optimizes recommendation quality also implicitly optimize user retention, maximize user population and bring about the system's long-term success? If yes, then the mainstream approach, discovering new learning algorithms that optimize some forms of recommendation quality, is justified. If not, then practitioners may not benefit from the most advanced learning algorithm.

Some notable exceptions in the reinforcement learning (RL) literature address the optimization of user retention without answering the above research question [3, 31, 32, 34]. However, these approaches do not discuss why explicitly optimizing retention is necessary. As [3] admit, "the relationship between retention reward and the intermediate feedback is not clear." Moreover, even though the RL literature acknowledges the importance of churn, it still ignores *user inflow*. Considering user inflow is obviously more faithful to the reality when we think about RS, but does it have any nontrivial implications that justify the extra complexity?

This paper differs from the existing literature by modeling the user as a flow and analyzing the system's equilibrium behavior. Conceptually, I demonstrate that the introduction of user inflow has profound and counterintuitive implications on how we think about improving recommendation algorithms. User inflow and churn are two competing forces that affect user population. When these two forces strike a balance, the system reaches a steady state in which the user distribution remains constant. However, the RS may take a long time to converge to this state. During this time, the system may differ significantly from its steady-state behavior.

Practically, I show that A/B testing after changing the recommendation algorithm may lead to biased test results. Changes in recommendation quality may alter user churn and disrupt the existing steady state. Because developers usually A/B test their systems shortly after making changes, they measure test metrics during the transition periods. These transitory metrics do not necessarily agree with their steady-state counterparts. More critically, changes that harm the system in the long run may seem beneficial in the A/B test.

The user inflow and churn dynamics also hints a new form of data bias in developing RS algorithms. In their excellent survey, [4] define data bias as the deviation from the underlying distribution. In this sense, the departure from the long-term steady-state distribution is also a data bias. Paradoxically, when a developer tries a new model architecture, she must train the new model using existing data, which is generally biased from the new architecture's steady state. What are the implications of this bias? How can it be mitigated? Given this paper's theoretical focus, I leave these questions to future research.

Related Work. Mainstream recommendation models generally can be framed as supervised learning problems where the ground-truth training labels are explicit user-item ratings or implicit feedback signals [17]. The goal is to accurately predict the training labels. Examples of general-purpose approaches include probabilistic matrix factorization [24], factorization machine [23], and neural factorization machine [13]. A slight reformulation of the problem aims to predict ranking as accurately as possible. Examples include [5,25,30]. For implicit feedback signals, scholars have tried click [19], purchase [15], dwell time [33], user engagement [7], cursor movement [12], etc. Within this literature, training labels are typically viewed as instantaneous signals directly linked to users' current behavior. Furthermore, this body of work often assumes either implicitly or explicitly that users form a fixed set or follow a fixed distribution. For example, [24] write: "Suppose we have M movies, N users..."; [30] write: "Assume that we have m items and u users"; [6] write: "Let U and I be the sets of users and items respectively, where the cardinalities $|U| = m$ and $|I| = n$."

A major exception that relaxes the assumption of the fixed user distribution is the RL literature. [3] develop an algorithm that directly minimizes the cumulative discounted return time. [31] propose a bandit-based solution to balance immediate feedback, future clicks, and exploration. [32] describe a residual learning approach to improve upon the deployed production policy. [34] devise a method to optimize a composite inter-temporal user engagement metric. In this literature, users can churn explicitly or implicitly through performing null actions. Nevertheless, this literature does not consider user inflow as an integral part of their modeling.

Many articles that explore new RS algorithms are susceptible to the pitfall identified in this paper. [6,14,18,23,24,32] show performance gains of their respective algorithms only on some fixed benchmark datasets. [31] retroactively compare their solution against a battery of baseline bandit algorithms on Yahoo news recommendation logs. [34] evaluate their method on two days' data after their training time window. [11] measure the first-week click-through rate and conversion rate after turning on the experiment as their A/B test metrics. [3] report live test metrics from day 0 to day 150 to claim superiority over their status quo. Even though their A/B test is much longer than others, it is unclear if 150 days are enough for their system to converge to the new steady state. [1] describe their offline-online testing procedure for RS innovations in Netflix. They write:

> Once offline testing has validated a hypothesis, we are ready to design and launch the online AB test that will demonstrate if an algorithmic change is an improvement from the perspective of user behavior. If it does, we will be ready to deploy the algorithmic improvement to the whole user-base.

However, according to this paper, it might be unwise to launch an online A/B test "once offline testing has validated a hypothesis" because Netflix's monthly billing model can cause their system taking a long time to converge.

The existing literature on RS bias largely focuses on counterfactual biases like feedback loop [20], selection bias [28], exposure bias [18], position bias [11,29], and so on. A recent comprehensive literature survey on biases in RS can be found at [4]. However, to the best of my knowledge, the bias caused by user inflow and churn dynamics had not been identified in the literature.

This paper also relates to the literature on user satisfaction with RS. [16] note that accuracy and diversity can influence user satisfaction in RS. [22] show that user personality contributes to their satisfaction with RS. Based on these empirical findings, I incorporate both recommendation quality and unobserved factors into the model setup discussed below, assuming they impact user retention.

2 Model Setup and the Status Quo

I consider a world where time is discrete and infinite. At the beginning of each period, a continuum of new users with unit mass arrive and start to consume the contents that an RS recommends. For simplicity, I assume that the new user distribution can be parameterized by two variables, x and e, and I use $F(x, e)$ to denote this distribution function. I assume x is an observable feature to the RS. The machine learning model behind the RS may use x to compute its predictions. In practice, x can represent self-reported user demographics, signals collected from past user behaviors, or data obtained from third-party vendors about users' general web activities. The variable e, however, is hidden from the RS and includes private user information relevant to RS consumption, such as personality, job, wealth, education level, and offline activities.

To further simplify the setup, I assume that x and e can each take only two values: $3/4$ or $1/4$. This creates four user types based on their (x, e) combinations. I also make the following symmetric distributional assumption: $F(x = 3/4, e = 3/4) = F(x = 1/4, e = 1/4) = \alpha$ and $F(x = 3/4, e = 1/4) = F(x = 1/4, e = 3/4) = 1/2 - \alpha$, where $\alpha \in (0, 1/2)$ is an exogenous parameter.

At the end of each period, each existing user decides whether to churn or not. Churn means the user stops using the RS. Once a user churns, they never return.[2] For the purpose of this paper, I abstract away the specific contents recommended by the RS. Instead, I assume that user's churn decision can be influenced by a statistic of items recommended during the period.[3] I interpret this statistic recommendation quality and denote it as q, where $q \in (0, 1)$. In the real world, the recommendation quality statistic may have many names. In an ad recommendation system, it may be the user-level click-through rate. In a movie recommendation system, it may be the view rate or completion rate. In an online shopping system, it may be the conversion rate.

As shown by empirical studies [8], different user segments may have different performance. Because x is an observable but e is not, q must be a function mapping from the feature set, $x \in \{1/4, 3/4\}$, to the recommendation quality statistic. This function summarizes the intricacies of a recommendation algorithm as a simple mapping. As the system only sees two segments of users, I call $x = 3/4$ the high segment and $x = 1/4$ low segment.

---

[2] In the real world, churned users may change their mind and come back, but in this model, they are treated as new users.

[3] Thus, recommendation quality is a short-term signal by assumption, aligning with the mainstream literature that uses short-term signals to train RS models.

Formally, I assume that a user who has not churned has a probability of $(1-q)(1-e)$ to churn at the end of the period. The term $(1-q)$ indicates that as the recommendation quality increases, the likelihood of user churn decreases. For $1-e$, it is known as the frailty term in the survival analysis literature [2]. The frailty term denotes user's unobserved heterogeneity that cannot be explained by observed covariates [22]. Higher e implies a healthier user, who is less likely to churn for reasons unobserved to the RS, and vice versa. A user who does not churn at the end of a period is called a retained user for that period.

The user distribution in the system may change over time due to user inflow and churn. It may also reach a stable point where user inflow and churn are balanced. This point is called the steady state, and is defined as follows.

Definition (Steady State). *The steady state of the system is an equilibrium point where user inflow fully offsets churned users at each period for each type. Formally, $m_\infty(x,e) \cdot \Pr(\text{churn}|x,e) = F(x,e)$ for all (x,e), where $m_\infty(x,e)$ is the population of type (x,e) users retained in the steady state.*

All steady-state quantities are subscripted by ∞. The steady-state user distribution can be obtained by $m_\infty(x,e) = F(x,e)/\Pr(\text{churn}|x,e)$.

Success Metrics. In our current setup, two metrics that measure the success of RS are naturally defined: *retained user population* and *average recommendation quality (ARQ)*. To assess the long-term success of the system, I focus on their steady-state values.

Steady State User Population. For many tech companies, getting more users and grow is a constant theme. Thus, I consider the user population retained in the steady-state, denoted as m_∞, the core metric to measure the RS success. Its real world counterpart is per-period (e.g., daily or monthly) active or paying user, which is considered a top-line metric by many real world RSs [10,21]. In our current setup, $m_\infty = \sum_x \sum_e m_\infty(x,e)$.

Average Recommendation Quality (ARQ). Developers may routinely track aggregated recommendation quality metrics like click-through rate, completion rate, or average rating. Arguably, these metrics are the most direct measures of an RS's performance. Therefore, developers may naturally focus on enhancing them. For example, a developer working on a video recommendation system might aim to boost the watch rate. Similarly, a developer of an ad recommendation system might consider the average click-through rate as a key metric. Using $\bar{q}$ to denote ARQ, we have $\bar{q}_\infty = \left(\sum_x q(x)(\sum_e m(x,e))\right) / \left(\sum_x \sum_e m(x,e)\right)$.

Status Quo. Suppose that the RS has been using an existing recommendation algorithm, called status quo, for a long time and has reached its steady state. I use $*$ to superscript quantities of the status quo. As all metrics in the status quo have reached their steady state values, I omit their ∞ subscripts to simplify notation. Normalizing $q^*(x) = x$ to be the recommendation quality function in the status quo, we can easily obtain $m^*(3/4, 3/4) = 16\alpha$, $m^*(3/4, 1/4) = m^*(1/4, 3/4) = 8(1 - 2\alpha)/3$, $m^*(1/4, 1/4) = 16\alpha/9$, $m^* = 16(4\alpha + 3)/9$, and $\bar{q}^* = (8\alpha + 3)/(8\alpha + 6)$.

3 Treatment Algorithm and A/B Experimentation

In this section, I consider a stereotypical situation where a developer aims to improve the recommendation algorithm and evaluates a treatment algorithm via an A/B test. An A/B test is a side-by-side comparative method that assesses two algorithms to determine which performs better. I use T to superscript quantities of the treatment. Given that $q^*(x)$ encapsulates the status quo recommendation algorithm, any enhancement to the current algorithm boils down to modifying this function. To simplify the notation, I define $q_3 \equiv q^T(3/4)$ and $q_1 \equiv q^T(1/4)$.

The steady-state behavior of the new algorithm can be studied immediately.

Proposition 1. *We have that* $m_\infty^T \geq (<) \, m^*$ *if and only if* $\bar{q}_\infty^T \geq (<) \, \bar{q}^*$.

All proofs can be found in the appendix. This proposition justifies the bedrock of the mainstream RS literature: optimizing for recommendation quality and gaining users are perfectly aligned in the long run. From now on, I use *steady-state performance* as a collective term to denote either of the steady state metrics.

However, Proposition 1 does not imply that A/B testing the treatment algorithm will always produce the correct outcome.

A/B Experimentation. Concretely, at the onset of some period, the treatment algorithm is implemented on a random subset of users. To simplify the discussion of experimental results, I assume that this subset is also a continuum that inherits all statistical properties of the existing user distribution. The A/B experimentation lasts for one period, to mirror the real-world scenario where A/B tests are typically much shorter than the longevity of the system. The developer collects data at the end of the period and makes a verdict between the status quo and the treatment.

I consider the following two metrics to measure the experiment success: ARQ and churn rate. Notice metrics observed in the experiment, subscripted with E, are generally different from their steady state counterparts. In our current setup,

$$\bar{q}_E^T = \frac{1}{m^*} \sum_x \left(q^T(x) \left(\sum_e m^*(x, e) \right) \right). \tag{1}$$

Churn Rate. Churn rate is the percentage of users who churn out of the total population of existing users during the experiment period. In some situations, the developer may directly monitor user churn. This could be because the developer understands that her work influences churn and does not want to lose users. It may also be that the developer cannot directly observe the recommendation quality and uses churn rate as a substitute. Using λ to denote churn rate, we have $\lambda^* = 1/m^*$ and

$$\lambda_E^T = \frac{1}{m^*} \sum_x \left((1 - q^T(x)) \left(\sum_e m^*(x,e)(1-e) \right) \right). \quad (2)$$

It is important to note that both (1) and (2) use the user distribution of the status quo. This is because the user distribution has not changed by the treatment algorithm yet when it is first introduced.

The following lemma suggests that ARQ and churn rate may provide contradicting signals to the experiment's success, despite optimizing for recommendation quality and gaining users are perfectly aligned in the long run.

Lemma 1. *If*

$$((4\alpha - 3)q_1 + 8\alpha + 3)/(12\alpha + 3) < q_3 < (5 - 2q_1)/6 \quad (3)$$

and either $q_1 < 1/4 < \alpha$ or $\alpha < 1/4 < q_1$ holds, then $\bar{q}_E^T > \bar{q}^*$ and $\lambda_E^T > \lambda^*$.

Practitioners may notice that quality metrics and churn do not always go hand in hand in reality. Lemma 1 provides a theoretical explanation. The driving force here is the frailty term $1-e$. Because of it, the marginal contributions of Δq_1 and Δq_3 to the hazard rate vary among user types. However, it does not affect the marginal contributions to ARQ. Thus, when q_1 and q_3 change by the "correct" amount, one metric may appear to improve while the other may seem to regress.

The following corollary summarizes the conditions under which the experiment is deemed a "success" by either metric. When it holds, it's reasonable to assume that the developer would favor the treatment over the status quo.

Corollary 1. *Suppose q_1 and q_3 satisfy either of the following conditions:*

1. *If $\alpha = 1/4$, $6q_3 + 2q_1 > 5$.*
2. *If $\alpha < 1/4$, $(q_1, q_3) \in \{(q_1, q_3) | q_1 \geq 1/4, 6q_3 + 2q_1 > 5\} \cup \{(q_1, q_3) | q_1 < 1/4, (12\alpha + 3)q_3 + (3 - 4\alpha)q_1 > 8\alpha + 3\}$.*
3. *If $\alpha > 1/4$, $(q_1, q_3) \in \{(q_1, q_3) | q_1 \leq 1/4, 6q_3 + 2q_1 > 5\} \cup \{(q_1, q_3) | q_1 > 1/4, (12\alpha + 3)q_3 + (3 - 4\alpha)q_1 > 8\alpha + 3\}$.*

The developer observes $\bar{q}_E^T > \bar{q}^*$ and $\lambda_E^T < \lambda^*$ in her experiment.

In A/B experiments, success metrics, regardless of their definitions, are generally computed based on existing users. A change to the recommendation algorithm may impact different user segments in varying ways, possibly altering the steady state. The system moves to its new steady state through user inflow and churn. Given that churn takes time to manifest, convergence to the new steady state can be a lengthy process. Thus, metrics based on existing users may not always provide insights into the system's future behavior. In fact, relying on such metrics could be misleading for the long-term success of the RS. The rest of the paper demonstrates this insight in detail.

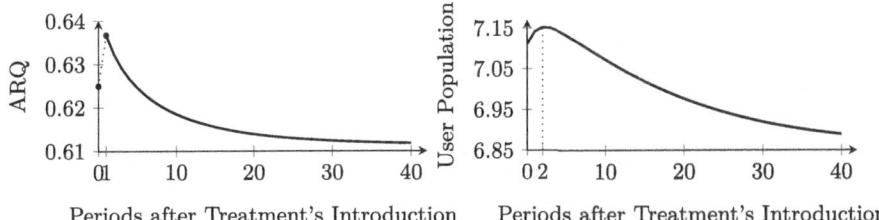

Fig. 1. ARQ and Population Dynamics after Introducing a Treatment Algorithm

Lemma 2 (ARQ Improvement). *When q_1 and q_3 satisfy*

$$(12\alpha + 3)q_3 + (3 - 4\alpha)q_1 > 8\alpha + 3 \tag{4}$$

and

$$(4\alpha + 1)/(1 - q_3) + (3 - 4\alpha)/(1 - q_1) < 8(4\alpha + 3)/3, \tag{5}$$

the developer observes $\overline{q}_E^T > \overline{q}^*$ in her experiment. However, $\overline{q}_\infty^T < \overline{q}^*$.

Remarkably, even though the developer observes an improvement in ARQ in the experiment, the new algorithm may decrease this quality in the long run. To further illustrate this point, consider a simulation where the developer applies a treatment algorithm with $q_1 = 7/16, q_3 = 45/64$ to all users in a system with $\alpha = 1/4$. The simulated ARQ path, plotted in the left panel of Fig. 1, shows that ARQ hikes following the introduction of the treatment. However, it gradually converges to its new steady state value, which is significantly lower than the status quo value.

Lemma 3 (Churn Reduction). *When q_1 and q_3 satisfy*

$$6q_3 + 2q_1 > 5 \tag{6}$$

and (5), the developer observes $\overline{\lambda}_E^T < \overline{\lambda}^*$ in her experiment. However, $m_\infty^T < m^*$.

That is, the developer may observe that more users are retained in the A/B test even if her new algorithm hurts the RS's ability to retain users in the long run.

The right panel of Fig. 1 plots the dynamics of the retained user population in the above simulation. It shows that user population increases for two periods after the treatment's introduction and then gradually declines and converges to the new steady state value. However, due to the initial increase, it remains above the status quo level until the seventh period.

Why can the RS retain more users to begin with? In the simulation, q_1 rises by 75%. This significant increase causes the low segment's new steady state to be considerably different from the status quo. As a result, this segment experiences a substantial user growth in the early periods. However, as the low segment's population converges, its growth slows down. On the other hand, q_3 decreases by only 6.25%. This is a relatively minor impact, which takes longer to manifest.

Nevertheless, the cumulative effect of this negative impact eventually surpasses the positive impact from the low segment since the high segment has a larger population to begin with. Consequently, we observe a short-term increase in user population, even though there is a permanent decline in the long run.

Combining Corollary 1, Lemma 3 and 2, we reach the core argument of this paper.

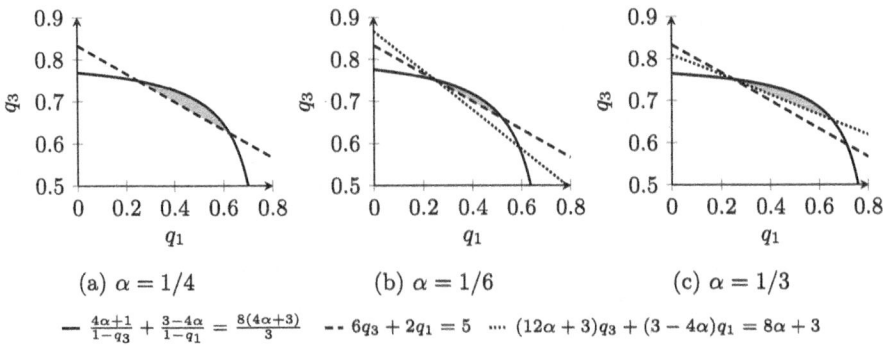

Fig. 2. Treatment Algorithms that Satisfy Proposition 2

Proposition 2 (Unequivocal Improvements). *Suppose either set of the following conditions holds:*

1. *If $\alpha > 1/4$, q_1 and q_3 satisfy (4) and (5).*
2. *If $\alpha \leq 1/4$, q_1 and q_3 satisfy (5) and (6).*

The developer observes $\bar{q}_E^T > \bar{q}^*$ and $\bar{\lambda}_E^T < \bar{\lambda}^*$. However, $\bar{q}_\infty^T < \bar{q}^*$ and $m_\infty^T < m^*$.

In other words, when q_1 and q_3 move by "right" amounts, the A/B experiment is considered a "success" by either metric but the treatment permanently impairs the RS performance in the long run.

Figure 2 plots the (q_1, q_3) pairs that satisfy Proposition 2, which may shed some light on the underlying mechanism. According to the figure, in order for the steady state metrics to stay constant, q_1 and q_3 must move along a concave curve (the solid lines). Conversely, to maintain either experimental metric neutral, q_1 and q_3 need only follow a straight line (the dotted or dashed lines). For all α, there exists a section of the solid curve that lies above both straight lines.

Why do q_1 and q_3 follow a concave curve to keep steady-state metrics constant, and why do they move along straight lines to maintain experimentation metrics neutral? Mathematically, the impacts of Δq_1 and Δq_3 enter the short-term experimentation metrics *linearly* because only one period is measured. However, the system is generally far from converged. From the second period onward, each segment's state lies between the original and the new steady state, causing the effects to diminish gradually. In fact, all subsequent periods contribute to the long term calculation *geometrically*. Since the horizon of the experimentation is finite, these cumulatively significant long-term effects are therefore overlooked.

As depicted in Fig. 2, for Proposition 2 to hold, the recommendation quality in the high segment only decreases mildly, while the low segment's recommendation quality improves significantly. In fact, the q_3 elasticity of q_1, formally defined as $-(\Delta q_1/q_1^*)/(\Delta q_3/q_3^*)$, is greater than 9 for all q_1 and q_3 that satisfy Proposition 2. Therefore, the intuition behind Lemma 3 generally applies: the more substantial improvement in the low segment has a more immediate impact, while the negative impact in the high segment materializes more slowly.

4 Research Implications and Limitations

Implications. This discovery has profound and disturbing implications in the real world. First, it questions the validity of the A/B testing paradigm in RS evaluation. A/B testing is often regarded the gold standard for determining the efficacy of RS [9]. Numerous authors and RS practitioners assert the superiority of their approaches by presenting results from side-by-side tests [26,27]. However, increases in recommendation quality metrics and retaining more users in A/B tests may merely indicate the system's bleak long-term successfulness.

Secondly, well-intentioned developers may inadvertently harm the system. For instance, a developer might aim to enhance the low segment's performance. However, improving the recommendation quality for one segment is not always free. For a new algorithm that significantly improves the low segment but causes a seemingly minor loss in the high segment, the algorithm might be deemed an improvement in an A/B test, despite its long-term detrimental impact. On the contrary, a nefarious developer may undermine the system by cooking up a series of sabotages under the guise of improvements.

Finally, to accurately assess the long term impacts of RS improvements, it is imperative for researchers to come up with a sophisticated experimental methodology in future studies. Questions arise such as: Should an experimentalist explicitly segment users? Is it necessary to measure system convergence? Most crucially, how can one forecast the long-term steady-state behavior from a sample with a finite horizon?

Limitations. Like all research, this piece is not without limitations. First, the findings are theoretical constructs from an idealized model, whereas real-world RSs can be affected by various noises, making it challenging to isolate retention induced biases from confounding factors. For empirical evidence that may support these theoretical findings, one may retroactively examine some natural experiments. In tech companies, restructurings due to exogenous reasons (e.g., leadership changes, layoffs, mergers) occasionally occur, disrupting RS teams. In such cases, the RS may only receive minimal maintenance, ceasing active development and naturally progressing towards its long-term state. If one can access data from these unfortunate cases, one may study the RS's real-world trajectory as it converges to its steady state.

The mechanism described here relies on two key assumptions: (1) an open system with free user inflow and churn, and (2) user churn stochastically related to recommendation quality. Thus, it doesn't apply to closed systems with fixed membership, like internal recommendation engines, or monopolistic platforms with inelastic demand. Additionally, the analysis pertains mainly to mature systems, as nascent systems in hyper-growth stages are too unstable to discuss steady states meaningfully.

The success of RS in this study is measured by the number of users. Even though it is not very controversy to assume that today's tech companies are interested in getting more users and grow, there may be exceptions. For example, because not all users generate the same amount of revenue, a revenue-maximizing stakeholder might forgo unprofitable users. This paper cannot analyze all conceivable success metrics. Nevertheless, the core principle that uneven churn leads to differences between short-term and long-term user distributions remains applicable to metrics related to users. Interested readers can use the framework presented here to analyze their own metrics.

Moreover, many real world RSs are constantly changing and some might never reach their steady states if changes are too frequent. Therefore, even though the findings here have theoretical importance on their own, one may question their practicability. For instance, can a developer constantly introduce short-term boosts (that are harmful in the long run) to indefinitely stall the downturn? This question merits further research.

5 Conclusion

This study examines a conceptual model of an RS, its developer, and its heterogeneous users. With the dynamics of user inflow and churn, the user distribution may achieve a steady state. When a new recommendation algorithm is introduced, the system moves away from its current steady state and begins transitioning to a new one, which can be a long process. However, the A/B test that validates the new algorithm is usually conducted shortly after the algorithm's development. During the transition period, the system's behavior can differ significantly from its steady state. Consequently, the metrics from A/B testing may provide misleading indicators of the new algorithm's long term success. This discrepancy is the live testing bias caused by user retention dynamics. In addition, retention dynamics can also introduce data bias for model training. Given the theoretical focus of this paper, examining data bias is reserved for future work.

Appendix

Lemma 4. *The following results hold:*

1. *For all α, $q_1 = 1/4, q_3 = 3/4$ satisfy $(12\alpha + 3)q_3 + (3 - 4\alpha)q_1 = 8\alpha + 3$ and $6q_3 + 2q_1 = 5$ simultaneously.*

2. When $\alpha = 1/4$, $(12\alpha + 3)q_3 + (3 - 4\alpha)q_1 = 8\alpha + 3$ and $6q_3 + 2q_1 = 5$ are equivalent.
3. (6) implies (4) if $\alpha < 1/4 \leq q_1$ or $q_1 \leq 1/4 < \alpha$.
4. (4) implies (6) if $\alpha < 1/4, q_1 < 1/4$ or $\alpha > 1/4, q_1 > 1/4$.

Proof. The first result can be obtained by plugging $q_1 = 1/4, q_3 = 3/4$ into $(12\alpha + 3)q_3 + (3 - 4\alpha)q_1 = 8\alpha + 3$ and $6q_3 + 2q_1 = 5$. The second result can be obtained by substituting α with $1/4$ in $(12\alpha + 3)q_3 + (3 - 4\alpha)q_1 = 8\alpha + 3$.

To prove the third result, notice $(12\alpha + 3)q_3 + (3 - 4\alpha)q_1 = (12\alpha + 3)q_3 + (4\alpha + 1)q_1 + (2 - 8\alpha)q_1$. By (6), $(12\alpha + 3)q_3 + (4\alpha + 1)q_1 > 5(4\alpha + 1)/2$. Therefore, $(12\alpha + 3)q_3 + (4\alpha + 1)q_1 + (2 - 8\alpha)q_1 > (2 - 8\alpha)q_1 + 5(4\alpha + 1)/2$. When $\alpha < 1/4 \leq q_1$ or $q_1 \leq 1/4 < \alpha$, $(2 - 8\alpha)q_1 \geq (2 - 8\alpha)/4$. In sum, we have $(12\alpha + 3)q_3 + (3 - 4\alpha)q_1 > (2 - 8\alpha)/4 + 5(4\alpha + 1)/2 = 8\alpha + 3$.

To show (6), it is sufficient to show $(12\alpha + 3)q_3 + (4\alpha + 1)q_1 > 5(4\alpha + 1)/2$. Notice $(12\alpha + 3)q_3 + (4\alpha + 1)q_1 = (12\alpha + 3)q_3 + (3 - 4\alpha)q_1 + (8\alpha - 2)q_1$. By (4), $(12\alpha + 3)q_3 + (3 - 4\alpha)q_1 > 8\alpha + 3$. When $\alpha < 1/4$ and $q_1 < 1/4$ or $\alpha > 1/4$ and $q_1 > 1/4$, $(8\alpha - 2)q_1 > (8\alpha - 2)/4$. Thus, $(12\alpha + 3)q_3 + (3 - 4\alpha)q_1 + (8\alpha - 2)q_1 > 10\alpha + 5/2$. □

Lemma 5. *If either (4) and (5) or (6) and (5) hold, we have $q_1 > 1/4$.*

Proof. For the first part, for a proof of contradiction, I assume that (4) and (5) hold for some $q_1 \leq 1/4$. Notice (5) can be rearranged as $q_3 < 1 - 3(4\alpha + 1)(1 - q_1)/(8(4\alpha + 3)(1 - q_1) - 3(3 - 4\alpha))$; (4) can be rearranged as $q_3 > ((8\alpha + 3) - (3 - 4\alpha)q_1)/(12\alpha + 3)$. For (4) and (5) to hold simultaneously, we must have $((8\alpha + 3) - (3 - 4\alpha)q_1)/(12\alpha + 3) < 1 - 3(4\alpha + 1)(1 - q_1)/(8(4\alpha + 3)(1 - q_1) - 3(3 - 4\alpha))$, which can be rearranged as $((3(4\alpha + 3))^2(1 - q_1) - (3 - 4\alpha)(44\alpha + 15 - (32\alpha + 34)q_1)q_1)/((44\alpha + 15) - (32\alpha + 24)q_1) < 4\alpha$. Because $q_1 \leq 1/4$, $(44\alpha + 15) - (32\alpha + 24)q_1 > 0$. Thus, we only require $8(3 + 4\alpha)q_1^2 - (40\alpha + 18)q_1 + 8\alpha + 3 < 0$. When $q_1 \leq 1/4$, its left hand side is monotonically decreasing with respect to q_1 and its minimal value is obtained at $q_1 = 1/4$, which is 0. Therefore, $8(3 + 4\alpha)q_1^2 - (40\alpha + 18)q_1 + 8\alpha + 3 \geq 0$ for all $q_1 \leq 1/4$, a contradiction.

For the second part, similarly, I assume that (5) and (6) hold for some $q_1 \leq 1/4$. For (5) and (6) to both hold, we must have $(5 - 2q_1)/6 < 1 - 3(4\alpha + 1)(1 - q_1)/(8(4\alpha + 3)(1 - q_1) - 3(3 - 4\alpha))$, which can be simplified to $(64\alpha + 48)q_1^2 - (128\alpha + 24)q_1 + 28\alpha + 3 < 0$. Following the same strategy above, a similar contradiction can be constructed. □

Proof of Proposition 1 Setting q_∞^T less (greater) than $\bar{q}^*$ yields $(4\alpha + 1)((8\alpha + 6)q_3 - (8\alpha + 3))/(1 - q_3) < (>)(3 - 4\alpha)((8\alpha + 3) - (8\alpha + 6)q_1)/(1 - q_1)$. Because $q_1, q_3 \in (0, 1)$, it can be further simplified to

$$-32\alpha q_1 q_3 + 20\alpha q_1 + 44\alpha q_3 - 24q_1 q_3 - 32\alpha + 21q_1 + 15q_3 - 12 < (>)0. \quad (7)$$

Similarly, setting $m_\infty^T = 2(4\alpha + 1)/(3(1 - q_3)) + 2(3 - 4\alpha)/(3(1 - q_1))$ less (greater) than m^* yields $(4\alpha + 1)/(1 - q_3) + (3 - 4\alpha)/(1 - q_1) < (>)8(4\alpha + 3)/3$. Because $q_1, q_3 \in (0, 1)$, it can be further simplified to

$$-32\alpha q_1 q_3/3 + 20\alpha q_1/3 + 44\alpha q_3/3 - 8q_1 q_3 - 32\alpha/3 + 7q_1 + 5q_3 - 4 < (>)0. \quad (8)$$

Notice (7) and (8) are identical except for a positive constant factor. □

Proof of Lemma 1 Plugging $m^*(x,e)$ into (1) yields $((12\alpha + 3)q_3 + (3 - 4\alpha)q_1)/(8\alpha + 6)$. Setting it greater than $(8\alpha + 3)/(8\alpha + 6)$ results (4). Similarly, plugging $m^*(x,e)$ into (2) and setting it greater than $1/m^*$ results $6q_3 + 2q_1 < 5$. Combining it with (4) results (3). For (3) to hold, a necessary condition is $(5 - 2q_1)/6 > ((4\alpha - 3)q_1 + 8\alpha + 3)/(12\alpha + 3)$, which simplifies to $(4\alpha - 1) > 4(4\alpha - 1)q_1$. Hence, (3) can possibly hold if and only if $q_1 < 1/4 < \alpha$ or $\alpha < 1/4 < q_1$. □

Proof of Corollary 1 Following similar steps in the proof of Lemma 1, one may reach that (4) is the condition for $\bar{q}_E^T > \bar{q}^*$ and (6) is the condition for $\lambda_E^T < \lambda^*$. Therefore, (4) and (6) must hold simultaneously here.

As shown in Lemma 4, (4) and (6) coincide when $\alpha = 1/4$, which proves the first part of Corollary 1. For the second and the third points, Lemma 4 shows that (4) is redundant if $\alpha < 1/4 \leq q_1$ or $q_1 \leq 1/4 < \alpha$ and (6) is redundant if $\alpha < 1/4, q_1 < 1/4$ or $\alpha > 1/4, q_1 > 1/4$. Finally, leaving out the redundant inequalities and rearranging terms yield the second and the third points. □

Proof of Lemma 2 As shown in previous proofs, (4) is the condition for $\bar{q}_E^T > \bar{q}^*$. Following the definition of m_∞, we have $m_\infty^T = (2(4\alpha + 1))/(3(1 - q_3)) + (2(3 - 4\alpha))/(3(1 - q_1))$. Setting it less than m^* yields (5).

To show the set

$$\left\{(q_1, q_3) \,\Big|\, (12\alpha + 3)q_3 + (3 - 4\alpha)q_1 > 8\alpha + 3, \frac{4\alpha + 1}{1 - q_3} + \frac{3 - 4\alpha}{1 - q_1} < \frac{8(4\alpha + 3)}{3}\right\} \quad (9)$$

is not empty, it is sufficient to find one element that belongs to it. For this, we may consider the case where $q_1 = (20\alpha + 9)/(32\alpha + 24)$ and $q_3 = (108\alpha + 63)/(128\alpha + 96)$. Plugging them into $(12\alpha+3)q_3+(3-4\alpha)q_1-(8\alpha+3)$ and $(4\alpha + 1)/(1 - q_3)+(3 - 4\alpha)/(1 - q_1) - 8(4\alpha + 3)/3$ yields $3(4\alpha + 1)(3 - 4\alpha)/(32(4\alpha + 3)) > 0$ and $-(16(4\alpha + 1)(4\alpha + 3)(3 - 4\alpha))/(3(4\alpha + 5)(20\alpha + 33)) < 0$ respectively. □

Proof of Lemma 3 As shown in previous proofs, (5) is the condition for $m_\infty^T < m^*$; (6) is the condition for $\lambda_E^T < \lambda^*$. Similar to the proof of Lemma 2, we need to show the set

$$\left\{(q_1, q_3) \,\Big|\, 6q_3 + 2q_1 > 5, \frac{4\alpha + 1}{1 - q_3} + \frac{3 - 4\alpha}{1 - q_1} < \frac{8(4\alpha + 3)}{3}\right\} \quad (10)$$

is not empty. To show it, plugging $q_1 = (16\alpha + 3)/(16\alpha + 12)$ and $q_3 = 3(16\alpha^2 + 20\alpha + 9)/(8\alpha + 6)^2$ into $6q_3 + 2q_1 - 5$ and $(4\alpha + 1)/(1 - q_3) + (3 - 4\alpha)/(1 - q_1) - 8(4\alpha + 3)/3$ yields $(24\alpha^2)/(4\alpha + 3)^2 > 0$ and $-(64\alpha^2(4\alpha + 3)^2)/(9(16\alpha^2 + 36\alpha + 9)) < 0$. □

Proof of Proposition 2 As shown in previous proofs, (4) is the condition for $\bar{q}_E^T > \bar{q}^*$; (5) is the condition for $m_\infty^T < m^*$; (6) is the condition for $\bar{\lambda}_E^T < \bar{\lambda}^*$. In order for Proposition 2 to hold, we need all (4) to (6) to hold simultaneously.

By Lemma 5, we have $q_1 > 1/4$ when either (4) and (5) or (5) and (6) hold. By Lemma 4, (4) implies (6) under $\alpha > 1/4$ and $q_1 > 1/4$. Therefore, $\alpha > 1/4$

and (4) and (5) are sufficient for (4) to (6) to hold. Similarly, (6) implies (4) under $\alpha < 1/4$ and $q_1 > 1/4$. Therefore, $\alpha < 1/4$ and (5) and (6) are sufficient for (4) to (6) to hold. Lastly, (4) and 6 coincide if $\alpha = 1/4$. □

References

1. Amatriain, X., Basilico, J.: Recommender systems in industry: a netflix case study. In: Recommender Systems Handbook. Springer (2015). https://doi.org/10.1007/978-1-4899-7637-6_11
2. Balan, T.A., Putter, H.: A tutorial on frailty models. Stat. Methods Med. Res. **29**(11), 3424–3454 (2020)
3. Cai, Q., et al.: Reinforcing user retention in a billion scale short video recommender system. In: ACM Web Conference 2023 - Companion of the World Wide Web Conference, WWW 2023 (2023)
4. Chen, J., Dong, H., Wang, X., Feng, F., Wang, M., He, X.: Bias and debias in recommender system: a survey and future directions. ACM Trans. Inf. Syst. **41**(3) (2023)
5. Chen, M., Zhou, X.: DeepRank: learning to rank with neural networks for recommendation. Knowl. Based Syst. **209**, 106478 (2020)
6. Cheng, P., Wang, S., Ma, J., Sun, J., Xiong, H.: Learning to recommend accurate and diverse items. In: 26th International World Wide Web Conference, WWW 2017 (2017)
7. Diaz-Aviles, E., et al.: Predicting user engagement in Twitter with collaborative ranking. In: Proceedings of the 2014 Recommender Systems Challenge, pp. 41–46 October 2014 (2014)
8. Erdem, E.E., Orman, G.K.: On the role of user segmentation in recommender systems' performances. Procedia Comput. Sci. **225**, 2333–2342 (2023)
9. Fabijan, A., Dmitriev, P., Arai, B., Drake, A., Kohlmeier, S., Kwong, A.: A/B integrations: 7 lessons learned from enabling A/B testing as a product feature. In: Proceedings - International Conference on Software Engineering (2023)
10. Facebook Inc.: Form 10-Q: Quarterly Report Pursuant to Section 13 or 15(d) of the Securities Exchange Act of 1934. Tech. rep. (2015). https://www.sec.gov/Archives/edgar/data/1326801/000132680115000015/fb-3312015x10q.htm
11. Guo, H., Yu, J., Liu, Q., Tang, R., Zhang, Y.: PAL: a position-bias aware learning framework for CTR prediction in live recommender systems. In: RecSys 2019 - 13th ACM Conference on Recommender Systems (2019)
12. Guo, Q., Agichtein, E.: Beyond dwell time: estimating document relevance from cursor movements and other post-click searcher behavior. In: WWW'12 - Proceedings of the 21st Annual Conference on World Wide Web (2012)
13. He, X., Chua, T.S.: Neural factorization machines for sparse predictive analytics. In: SIGIR 2017 - Proceedings of the 40th International ACM SIGIR Conference on Research and Development in Information Retrieval (2017)
14. Hidasi, B., Karatzoglou, A., Baltrunas, L., Tikk, D.: Session-based recommendations with recurrent neural networks. In: 4th International Conference on Learning Representations, ICLR 2016 - Conference Track Proceedings (2016)
15. Huang, C., Zhang, C., Wu, X., Zhao, J., Yin, D., Zhang, X., Chawla, N.V.: Online purchase prediction via multi-scale modeling of behavior dynamics. In: Proceedings of the ACM SIGKDD International Conference on Knowledge Discovery and Data Mining (2019)

16. Kim, J.K., Choi, I.Y., Li, Q.: Customer satisfaction of recommender system: Examining accuracy and diversity in several types of recommendation approaches. Sustainability (Switzerland) **13**(11), 6165 (2021)
17. Koren, Y., Bell, R., Volinsky, C.: Matrix factorization techniques for recommender systems. Computer **42**(8), 30–37 (2009)
18. Liang, D., Charlin, L., McInerney, J., Blei, D.M.: Modeling user exposure in recommendation. In: 25th International World Wide Web Conference, WWW 2016, pp. 951–961. International World Wide Web Conferences Steering Committee (2016)
19. Liu, J., Dolan, P., Pedersen, E.R.: Personalized news recommendation based on click behavior. In: International Conference on Intelligent User Interfaces, Proceedings IUI (2010)
20. Mansoury, M., Abdollahpouri, H., Pechenizkiy, M., Mobasher, B., Burke, R.: Feedback loop and bias amplification in recommender systems. In: International Conference on Information and Knowledge Management, Proceedings (2020)
21. Murariu, C.: Active Users: measuring Business Success with DAU, WAU, and MAU (2023). https://www.innertrends.com/blog/active-users-measuring-business-success-with-dau-wau-and-mau
22. Nguyen, T.T., Maxwell Harper, F., Terveen, L., Konstan, J.A.: User personality and user satisfaction with recommender systems. Inf. Syst. Frontiers **20**(6), 1173–1189 (2018)
23. Rendle, S.: Factorization machines. In: Proceedings - IEEE International Conference on Data Mining, ICDM (2010)
24. Salakhutdinov, R., Mnih, A.: Probabilistic matrix factorization. In: Advances in Neural Information Processing Systems 20 - Proceedings of the 2007 Conference (2008)
25. Shi, Y., Larson, M., Hanjalic, A.: List-wise learning to rank with matrix factorization for collaborative filtering. In: RecSys'10 - Proceedings of the 4th ACM Conference on Recommender Systems (2010)
26. Soria, L.L.: Using A/B testing to measure the efficacy of recommendations generated by Amazon Personalize (8 2020). https://aws.amazon.com/blogs/machine-learning/using-a-b-testing-to-measure-the-efficacy-of-recommendations-generated-by-amazon-personalize/
27. Vas, G.: Behind the Scenes of A/B Testing Recommendation Systems (9 2021), https://www.yusp.com/blog-posts/behind-the-scenes-of-ab-testing-recommendation-systems/
28. Wang, X., Bendersky, M., Metzler, D., Najork, M.: Learning to rank with selection bias in personal search. In: SIGIR 2016 - Proceedings of the 39th International ACM SIGIR Conference on Research and Development in Information Retrieval (2016)
29. Wang, X., Golbandi, N., Bendersky, M., Metzler, D., Najork, M.: Position bias estimation for unbiased learning to rank in personal search. In: WSDM 2018 - Proceedings of the 11th ACM International Conference on Web Search and Data Mining, vol. 2018, Febuary (2018)
30. Weimer, M., Karatzoglou, A., Viet Le, Q., Smola, A.: CoFiRANK maximum margin matrix factorization for collaborative ranking. In: Advances in Neural Information Processing Systems 20 - Proceedings of the 2007 Conference (2008)
31. Wu, Q., Wang, H., Hong, L., Shi, Y.: Returning is believing: optimizing long-term user engagement in recommender systems. In: International Conference on Information and Knowledge Management, Proceedings, vol. Part F131841 (2017)

32. Xue, W., Cai, Q., Zhan, R., Zheng, D., Jiang, P., Gai, K., An, B.: ResAct: reinforcing Long-term Engagement in Sequential Recommendation with Residual Actor. arXiv preprint arXiv:2206.02620 (2022)
33. Yi, X., Hong, L., Zhong, E., Liu, N.N., Rajan, S.: Beyond clicks: dwell time for personalization. In: RecSys 2014 - Proceedings of the 8th ACM Conference on Recommender Systems (2014)
34. Zou, L., Song, J., Xia, L., Liu, W., Ding, Z., Yin, D.: Reinforcement learning to optimize long-term user engagement in recommender systems. In: Proceedings of the ACM SIGKDD International Conference on Knowledge Discovery and Data Mining (2019)

Political Bias of Large Language Models in Few-Shot News Summarization

Takeshi Onishi[1]($\boxtimes$) and James Caverlee[2]

[1] Frontier Research Center, Toyota Motor Corporation, Toyota, Japan
Takeshi.Onishi@cshs.org
[2] Department of Computer Science and Engineering, Texas A&M University, College Station, USA
caverlee@tamu.edu

Abstract. As Large Language Models (LLMs) have become robust and universal in various tasks and increasingly popular and widely used in society, their political bias is becoming more and more critical. Hence, to probe the political bias of LLMs, several studies have proposed frameworks that ask political questions and estimate the political stance of LLMs by using their answers. However, these approaches suffer from the effect of the question's wording and the randomness of answer generation algorithms, and do not take into account information selection bias in the context of summarization tasks. In this work, we summarize news articles describing the same news event with different political stances by using the LLMs and evaluate the political stance of the output summaries by comparing the output and input texts. We probed some LLMs and found a potential political bias in word choice. Additionally, our result indicates that the bias can be mostly dissipated by generation algorithms.

1 Introduction

In recent years, Large Language Models (LLMs) have become ubiquitous foundation models in various natural language processing tasks, with applications ranging from natural language understanding to text generation. One of the most extensive fields to which LLMs are widely applied might be information retrieval and summarization. LLMs can comprehend large volumes of text and produce concise summaries [13]. Then this capability has enabled web search engines like Google and Bing, the two biggest web search engine sites, to offer summaries of retrieved information as part of their search results for each user [20,21]. However, LLMs with bias may cherry-pick information and provide a biased summary that reflects their bias, potentially influencing public opinion. Therefore, it is crucial for us to closely examine and address the biases in LLMs as they have a significant impact on society.

This work has been done during his visiting scholar program at Texas A&M University from Toyota Motor Corporation.

There are several studies that evaluate the bias of LLMs [9, 17]. Within existing frameworks, LLMs typically operate by utilizing templates or questions relating to bias attributes such as gender or politics, subsequently assessing the generated output texts. However, these frameworks relying on such templates or questions encounter three primary concerns. Firstly, there exists apprehension regarding the influence of prompts, whereby the phrasing of templates and questions may impact the bias exhibited by LLMs due to their sensitivity to prompts. For example, minor phrasing differences – such as using "write a summary" versus "summarize" – can occasionally impact the output. Additionally, the template style, like JSON versus HTML, can also affect performance. Secondly, the generation process entails inherent randomness, whereby algorithms for text generation seldom converge upon the optimal word sequence, thus leading to potential deviations from faithfully representing LLM biases in the generated texts. Lastly, there is a notable concern regarding information selection bias. As these frameworks provide simple prompts for the input, LLMs draw upon stored topic knowledge encoded within their parameters to expound upon the subject matter. Nevertheless, the process by which LLMs prioritize information gleaned from the input remains opaque, posing a significant challenge, particularly in the context of summarization tasks.

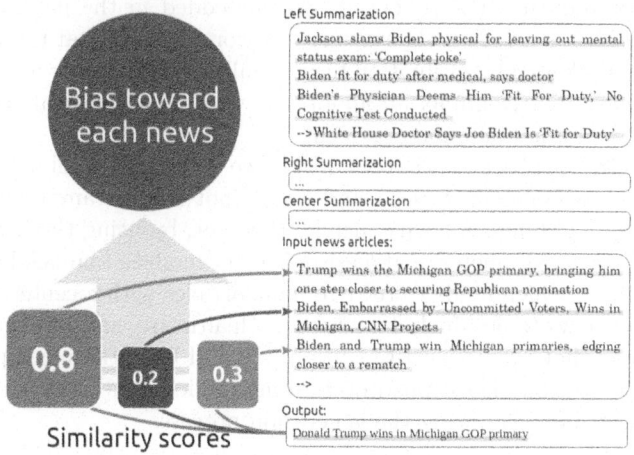

Fig. 1. The overview of our bias evaluation framework based on a news summarization task. An LLM takes left, right, and center summarizations as demonstrations, along with a set of left/right/center target news articles describing the same event with different political stances to be summarized. Eventually, we compare the generated summary with each target news article to ensure that the LLM utilizes information from all target news articles evenly. This framework does not rely on any natural language instructions to command the LLM.

In order to address these concerns, we study, in this paper, political bias in generated summaries without relying on templates or specific political bias attributes. We conducted an investigation into the political stances prioritized by LLMs among given input texts by comparing the input texts with specific political stances and the generated output text without any prompts, which potentially affects LLMs' bias. Here, we define the political bias in the context of summarization by the similarities among output and input texts, assuming that in the absence of any inherent political bias, an LLM would exhibit a uniform resemblance to all political stances present within the input text. Concretely, we propose a framework in a few-shot summarization setting that allows us to probe the political stance of LLMs. Instead of using prompts that potentially affect the political stance of LLMs, we designed the few-shot demonstrations, which show all possible political shifts in the summarization so that the demonstration describes the summarization task without any political shift in total. In our framework, an LLM summarizes a set of texts that describe the same news event but have different political stances, and we evaluate the similarities between the output summary and each input text. As our assumption, these similarities are uniform if the LLM has no bias; otherwise, the LLM might select more information from an input text with a specific political stance that the LLM prefers, making the similarity with the particular input text more prominent. We use the n-gram matching metric, ROUGE, as well as the likelihood where each political stance is selected as the summary for the similarity metric. The likelihood indicates the potential bias embedded in the parameter of the LLM regardless of generation algorithms. It is worth noting that these similarity metrics are not affected by evaluation biases, unlike classifying or annotating the output summary. For example, an annotator with a left political stance might tend to label a non-left summary as right.

Surprisingly, we observed that all LLMs we employed exhibited a uniform resemblance to all political stances, and we did not observe any political stance on the n-gram matching similarity metric. However, by using the likelihood, we discovered that the parameter of at least one of our models, Llama2, had a potential political bias, which tends to refer to news articles with a centering political stance in some news topics, including Justice, Healthcare, and Immigration. The result indicates that even if an LLM has a political bias, the incompleteness of sequence optimization algorithms injects some randomness into the word selection and covers the bias during the generation process.

2 Related Work

Textual information is a primary cue to probe the political stance of its authors, such as individual users and news sources. Microblogs like tweets can be a primary source to predict the political stance of the individual users [7,19,22], and political statements are used to estimate the political perspective of each politician [10]. Hence, news articles were also used to prove the political stance of the news source [8,18,24].

On the other hand, as pre-trained machine learning models are widely used in various downstream tasks and deployed as services, the political stance of these machine learning models is significantly critical for society and thus has been actively studied [1,2,11,14,16,23,25]. There are also researches to measure the political stance of these models and various components such as word embeddings [3,5,6,12,15], and output probability [4] in the context of text classification.

In the context of LLMs, several studies have proposed frameworks to evaluate the political stance of LLMs [9,17]. One such framework was proposed by Liu et al. (2021), where an LLM generates a text following a templated input with a specific attribute, such as gender, and then the generated text is evaluated to see if the attribute affects the output. Another study by Feng et al. (2023) showed the impact of pre-training data on the political stance of LLMs by questioning several LLMs. However, these studies are limited to dialog or question answering and suffer from the effect of word choice of the questions, and then it is not clear how the LLMs pick political stances of textual information when it summarizes.

3 Methodology

In this section, we introduce our bias evaluation framework, which is based on a news summarization task. In this framework, we used tuples of news articles describing the same news event but with different political stances. Considering the political spectrum from conservative to liberal, we focus on news articles from left, center, and right news sources. We let news articles describing the event from a left/center/right news source be l, c, r individually. Additionally, we have a professionally written politically neutral news article denoted as n. Each article from a left/center/right/neutral news source is expected to have the left/center/right/neutral political stance. Hence, we input a set of left/center/right target news articles, l, c, r, to be summarized along with other sets of left/center/right/neutral news articles as demonstrations into an LLM. Then, we compare the similarity between the generated summary and each target news article to see if the LLM takes information from all target news articles evenly.

3.1 Task

We leverage a few-shot summarization task: multi-target summarization. The task is to summarize a set of target news articles describing the same event into a single article by referring to three types of demonstrations: left summarization, right summarization, and center summarization. In the left summarization, the demonstration shows the transformation from a set of $\{r', c', n'\}$ to l'. In the same manner the right summarization and center summarization show transformation to r' and c' from others. A set of demonstrations to be provided to an LLM consists of the same number of the left, right, and center summarizations. Although each left/right/center summarization demonstrates a different political shift for each other, the entire set of demonstrations does not indicate any political shift. Along with the demonstrations, a set of target news articles describing the same event but with different political stances, i.e., $\{r, c, l\}$, is provided to be summarized. As you can see on the overview in Fig. 1, the LLM takes the demonstrations where a single special token separates each pair of input and output articles, and the set of target news articles followed by the special token to lead the summary. Hence, the framework does not rely on any natural language instruction to describe the summarization task. It is also worth noting that the order of input news articles and the demonstrations are shuffled with each generation to prevent summarization biases based on the position of input texts.

3.2 Measuring the Political Bias of LLMs

In this section, we explain how we estimated the political stance of each LLM in our summarization task. To determine the political stance of the LLMs, we assumed that an LLM would use more words and phrases from a given news article if the article had the same political stance as that of the LLM.

On the assumption, we employed two evaluation metrics: ROUGE score and posterior likelihood. The ROUGE score is a standard text similarity score between sentences in the machine translation. We compare the ROUGE score between the generated output text and each target news article from the left/center/right news source. As the ROUGE score only compares n-grams in the generated text and each target news article, it may not fully capture the political stance embedded in the LLM's parameters. Therefore, we also used another evaluation metric based on embedding, posterior likelihood.

The posterior likelihood is a probability where an LLM takes demonstrations and target news articles and then generates a complete copy of a target news article as its output, e.g.,

$$P_\theta(r|l, c, r, D) \tag{1}$$

where D is a set of given demonstrations and θ is model parameters. The posterior likelihood of each target news article indicates how likely the LLM is to selectively summarize the target news articles by using the news article. Additionally, as Fig. 4 shows, the posterior likelihoods of the input news articles are mostly higher than the likelihood of generated texts in our tasks. Although, in practice, LLMs rarely repeat a news article from the input because generation algorithms can only find the optimum sequence, the posterior likelihoods show the potential political bias of the LLM without the effect of generation algorithms.

4 Experiment

For our experiments, we crawled Allsides.com[1] for the dataset and probed two locally operated LLMs, Llama2 and Mistral, and one API-based LLM, GPT-3.5-Turbo.

---

[1] https://www.allsides.com.

Table 1. Sample headlines from Allsides.com and the average number of tokens for each political stance.

Stance	# of tokens per text		Sample Headline (news source)
	Headline	First Snt.	
Right	12.7	38.9	Jackson slams Biden physical for leaving out mental status exam: 'Complete joke' (Washington Examiner)
Center	11.3	38.3	Biden 'fit for duty' after medical, says doctor (BBC News)
Left	12.6	42.0	White House Doctor Says Joe Biden Is 'Fit for Duty' (Daily Beast)
Neutral	9.1	29.9	Biden's Physician Deems Him 'Fit For Duty,' No Cognitive Test Conducted (Allsides)

Table 2. Average ROUGE scores among news articles from different news sources. Each score is computed between a target news article and other articles from different news sources in the same news event, e.g., when the target news source is Left, ROUGE scores are computed for each pair of (l, r), (l, c), and (l, n), and then averaged.

	ROUGE score	
	Headline	First sent.
Left × others	0.265	0.179
Center × others	0.278	0.184
Right × others	0.263	0.183
Neutral × others	0.314	0.124

4.1 Dataset

We collected news articles from Allsides.com, a news website providing news articles from different news sources for each news event as Table 1. Each news source has its own political stance, Media Bias Ratings[2], estimated by panelist reviews and blind bias surveys. For example, the Media Bias Rating of CNN News is −4.0, and its political stance is considered to be on the left side. We crawled news events from August 2012 to December 2023.

To focus on each article's political stance and avoid other noisy information, we decided to use two parts of each news article – its headline and its first sentence. As we looked through the news articles, we found headlines tend to describe the news event directly and briefly since they have a limited length. Hence, they also tend to feature the same entities, such as the names of people or events, in any political stance, and each political stance is often conveyed through word choice (lexical bias). The first sentences also tend to describe the essential part of the news event; however, the first sentences have no length

---
[2] https://www.allsides.com/media-bias/ratings.

Table 3. Three class (Right/Center/Left) classification accuracies of news articles embedded by Llama2. The headlines and first sentences of the articles are embedded and classified independently.

	Headline	First Sentence
Logistic	0.46	0.50
MLP	0.47	0.48
SVM	0.51	0.54

Table 4. Topics and # of news events

	# of event
Education	65
Abortion	69
Justice	72
Gun Control And Gun Rights	74
Healthcare	75
Joe Biden	105
Violence In America	109
Presidential Elections	130
Immigration	169
Donald Trump	173
Economy And Jobs	231
Total # of events	5105

limitation, which allows the author to use more diverse entities, phrases, and even different aspects of the event. As a result, each political stance is typically represented by the selection of information (layout bias). We can see it in Table 5 and Table 6 for reference.

We briefly compare the statistical and lexical differences between the headlines and the first sentences. As Table 1 shows, the headlines are shorter than the first sentences. Additionally, Table 2 shows that the ROUGE scores among headlines are higher than the scores among the first sentences, it indicates that the headlines are shorter and lexically less diverse, and the first sentences are longer and more lexically diverse.

Furthermore, to see the political stance represented by the articles, we show the classification scores in Table 3. In this classification, we embedded news articles by an LLM and trained simple classifiers that take the embedding and predict its news source. We hypothesize that if the article embeddings do not reflect any political stance of news sources, then the classifiers would randomly classify the articles, resulting in an accuracy of one-third, as we have three equally distributed classes (left/right/center). However, the classification accuracies are

Table 5. Sample output of Llama2

Stance	Headline
Right	Trump refuses to admit 2020 election defeat in CNN town hall
Center	Trump refuses to say 2020 election wasn't rigged at CNN town hall
Left	Trump digs in on false election claims, defending Jan. 6 riot in CNN town hall
Output	Trump denies election fraud claims at CNN town hall, ignites controversy

Table 6. The first sentences of headlines in Table 5

Stance	First Sentence
Right	Former President Donald Trump addressed the nation in a CNN town hall on Wednesday. The event started with Trump refusing to admit a loss in the 2020 election.
Center	Former President Trump refused to acknowledge that the 2020 presidential election was not rigged while taking questions at a CNN town hall in New Hampshire on Wednesday.
Left	Former president Donald Trump kicked off his highly publicized return to mainstream prime time TV by repeatedly refusing to accept his defeat in the 2020 election and defending the mob of his supporters who disrupted the peaceful transfer of power.

around 50%, which indicates that each part of the news article has a detectable political stance, and they can be captured by the LLM embeddings.

We targeted eleven controversial news topics and collected news events on each topic with articles from left, right, and center news sources. Table 4 shows the topics and number of events for each topic. For each topic, we sampled two left, right, and center demonstrations within the same topic for each summarization, i.e., six news events for demonstrations in total and one target news event to be summarized for the input.

4.2 Large Language Model

We evaluated three popular LLMs: locally operated Llama2-7B and Mistral-7B and also API-based GPT-3.5-Turbo. Llama2 and Mistral are popular LLMs whose parameters are publicly available, so they are suitable for probing parameter details. On the other hand, GPT-3.5-Turbo is only available through API, but it is larger than other models, and its performance is expected to be better than the other two.

5 Result and Analysis

The charts shown in Fig. 2 present the average ROUGE scores calculated for different topics across different LLMs. Each point on the chart represents the average ROUGE score between the output summaries and the target news articles with a specific political stance for a particular news topic. If the points fall outside of the chart, it indicates that the output summaries are similar to the target articles and the quality of the summary is high. These points on the charts demonstrate that GPT-3.5 performs better than Llama2 and Mistral in this summarization task. Furthermore, we observed that the performance of Llama2 and Mistral differs for each news topic, and they sometimes generate nonsensical output (such as a single word or repetition) in some topics, unlike GPT-3.5. It's worth noting that the parameter size of GPT-3.5 is much larger than the other two models.

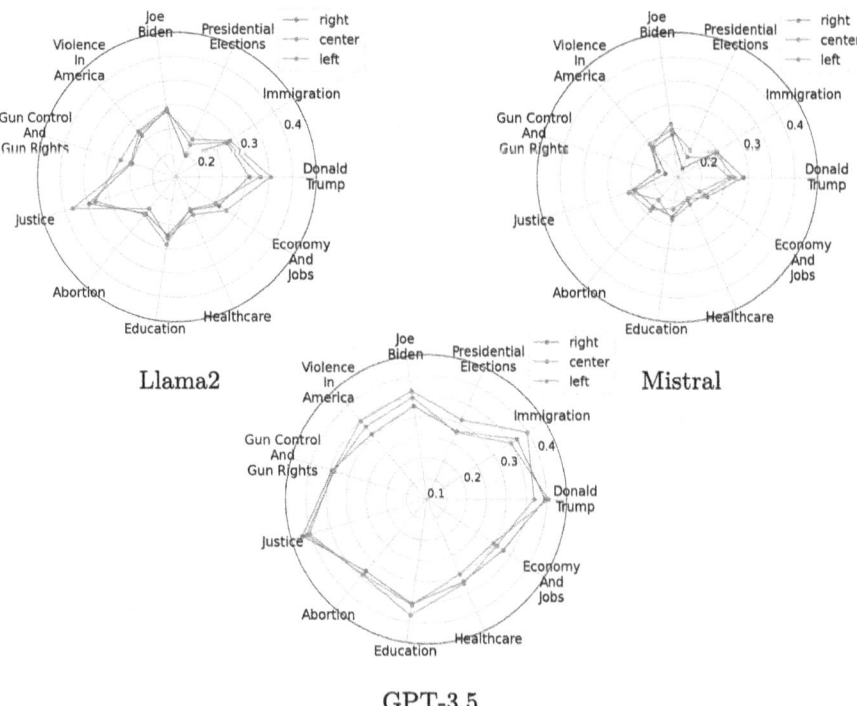

Fig. 2. ROUGE scores between generated text and input headlines in the multi-target summarization task. The ROUGE scores are averaged for each topic, and their colors indicate the average ROUGE score of each news source for each topic. The points go outside if the output text is more similar to the news source. The curves should lay on top of each other if there is no bias.

Furthermore, as Table 2 shows, the ROUGE scores among news sources remain below 0.30. As comparing ROUGE scores in Fig. 2, which are mostly more than 0.30, the quality of the output summaries is notably high. This observation suggests a challenge in distinguishing between the original inputs and the generated output. A sample output is in Table 5 for reference. Additionally, Fig. 3 delineates the distributions of these ROUGE scores. It is noteworthy that these distributions exhibit considerable deviations without manifesting any discernible biases towards particular news sources.

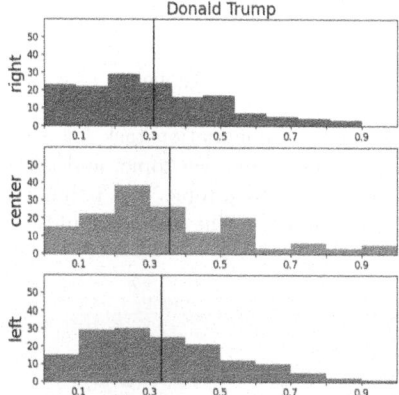

Fig. 3. The distribution of ROUGE scores by Llama2 in the topic of "Donald Trump".

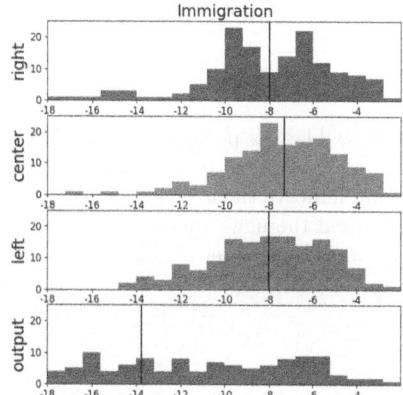

Fig. 4. The distribution of log posterior likelihoods by Llama2 in the topic of "Immigration"

In contrast, Fig. 5 (Headlines) shows the average posterior likelihoods for each topic. As the posterior likelihoods of target articles with a centering political stance are significantly higher than others on some topics such as Justice, Healthcare, and Immigration, Llama2 tends to summarize news articles by referring to the target news article with centering political stance more, and it seems Llama2 has a centering political stance. Additionally, Fig. 4 presents the distributions of the posterior likelihoods. Here, the posterior likelihood of actual output texts is significantly smaller than that of target articles (likelihood where one of the target news articles is repeated). It indicates that the target news articles are likely to have been summarized using extractive summarization; however, the actual output text generated by the algorithm is suboptimal.

We also see the summarization bias in first sentences in Fig. 5 (First sentences). We even found significant likelihood differences in some topics; however, the biases differ from those on headlines. The result indicates that LLMs have different political stances in lexical and layout bias, e.g., an LLM might choose words like a left news source but select information like a right news source.

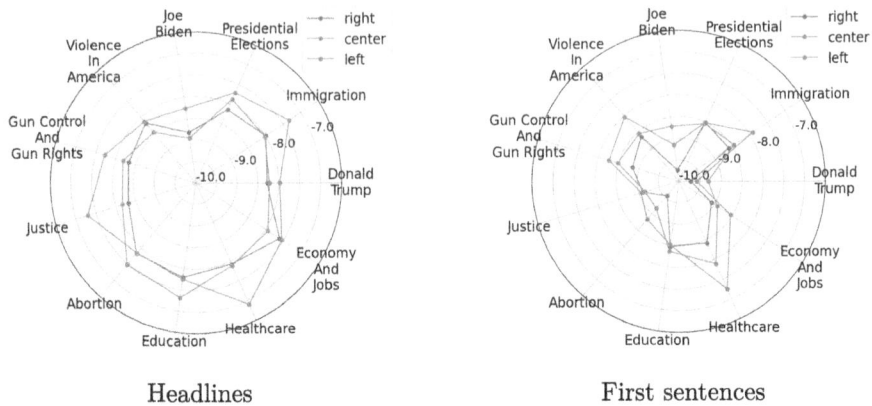

Fig. 5. The log posterior likelihood in the multi-target summarization task for each input news article by Llama2. The likelihoods are averaged for each topic, and their colors indicate the average likelihood of each news source for each topic. The points go outside if the news source tends to be selected as the summary. The curves should lay on top of each other if there is no bias.

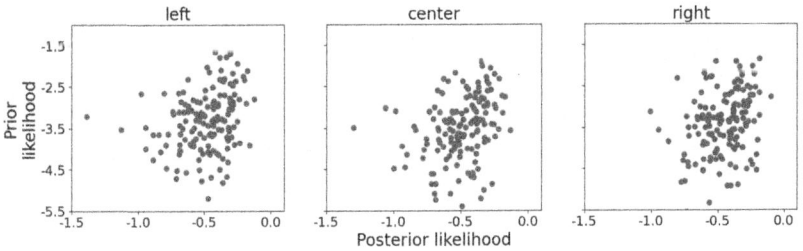

Fig. 6. Correlation between log posterior likelihood and log prior likelihood by Llama2.

To see the origin of the above summarization bias, we analyzed the relationship between the posterior likelihood and prior likelihood of each news article, as shown in Fig. 6. The prior likelihood is the likelihood where a news article is generated without any demonstrations or target articles, e.g., $P_\theta(r)$. Our findings indicate that there is a correlation between the two, but it's worth noting that the prior likelihood does not always determine the posterior likelihood. The posterior likelihood is also heavily influenced by other target news articles and demonstrations.

In our analysis, we observed that the likelihoods of the target news articles are higher than the likelihoods of the generated texts. We conducted an experiment where we examined the possibility of the generation algorithm producing suboptimal output texts due to its inability to capture the target news articles with higher likelihoods. Then, Fig. 7 demonstrates that the posterior likelihood of each token on the right part (end of the sentence) is higher than the prior likelihood on the same part, and the posterior likelihood on the left part (begin-

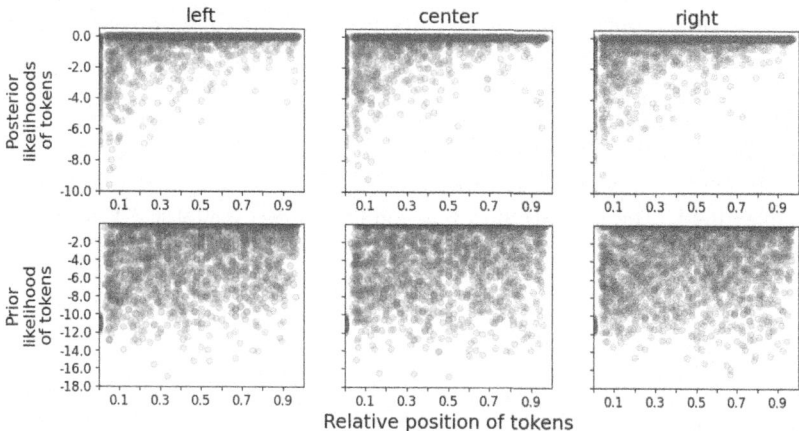

Fig. 7. Log likelihoods of each token in the multi-target summarization task by Llama2. Three charts on the first row show the posterior likelihood of each news source individually, and the other three charts on the bottom show the prior likelihood. Each dot indicates the likelihood of each token in the relative position.

ning of the sentence) is lower than that of the right part. Hence, the entropy over words at the left part is high. As the algorithm generates the output text by using the posterior probabilities of the tokens from the left, the higher entropy at the beginning of the generation process makes it difficult to find the optimum tokens. In other words, to generate the target news article with a high posterior likelihood, the generation algorithm must choose the first few tokens with low posterior likelihoods, which may likely result in the algorithm's inability to capture the target news effectively.

6 Conclusion

Our research focused on investigating the political bias of LLMs in the context of the summarization task. We accomplished this by using news articles that describe the same news event but present different political stances. Our framework involved providing an LLM with a set of such news articles as demonstrations and another set of target news articles to be summarized. We then compared the output summary with the target news articles. Unlike the existing evaluation frameworks that rely on questions or templates, our framework did not rely on any additional information, thus providing a more robust way to probe the bias of LLMs.

We found little bias when we compared them by shallow n-gram matching, i.e., ROUGE scores; however, we found a potential bias by posterior likelihoods. Additionally, a posterior likelihood where an input news article is repeated is higher than the likelihood of the text actually being generated. This indicates that the potential political bias of LLMs is small enough to be covered by the randomness of generation algorithms. We also saw the different political biases in different parts of news articles: headline and first sentence, and the biases are not consistent. The result indicates that LLMs might have different political stances in selecting an aspect of the news event (layout bias) and choosing words to describe the event (lexical bias) when they summarize.

The model scale is the first future work because our work is limited in the model size due to the limitation of our computational resources. We also desire to investigate the origin of the news source bias we found.

References

1. Bender, E.M., Gebru, T., McMillan-Major, A., Shmitchell, S.: On the dangers of stochastic parrots: can language models be too big? In: Proceedings of the 2021 ACM Conference on Fairness, Accountability, and Transparency (2021)
2. Blodgett, S.L., Barocas, S., Daumé III, H., Wallach, H.: Language (technology) is power: a critical survey of "bias" in NLP. In: Proceedings of the 58th Annual Meeting of the Association for Computational Linguistics (2020)
3. Bolukbasi, T., Chang, K.W., Zou, J.Y., Saligrama, V., Kalai, A.T.: Man is to computer programmer as woman is to homemaker? debiasing word embeddings. In: Proceedings of Advances in Neural Information Processing Systems (2016)
4. Borkan, D., Dixon, L., Sorensen, J., Thain, N., Vasserman, L.: Nuanced metrics for measuring unintended bias with real data for text classification. In: Companion Proceedings of the 2019 World Wide Web Conference, NY, U.S. (2019)
5. Caliskan, A., Bryson, J.J., Narayanan, A.: Semantics derived automatically from language corpora contain human-like biases. Science **356**(6334), 183–186 (2017)
6. Cao, Y., et al.: On the intrinsic and extrinsic fairness evaluation metrics for contextualized language representations. In: Proceedings of the 60th Annual Meeting of the Association for Computational Linguistics, Dublin, United Kingdom (2022)
7. Colleoni, E., Rozza, A., Arvidsson, A.: Echo chamber or public sphere? Predicting political orientation and measuring political homophily in Twitter using big data. J. Commun. **64**(2), 317–332 (2014)
8. Feng, S., et al.: KGAP: knowledge graph augmented political perspective detection in news media. arXiv preprint arXiv:2108.03861 (2021)
9. Feng, S., Park, C.Y., Liu, Y., Tsvetkov, Y.: From pretraining data to language models to downstream tasks: Tracking the trails of political biases leading to unfair NLP models. In: Rogers, A., Boyd-Graber, J., Okazaki, N. (eds.) Proceedings of the 61st Annual Meeting of the Association for Computational Linguistics, Toronto, Canada (2023)
10. Feng, S., et al.: PAR: political actor representation learning with social context and expert knowledge. In: Proceedings of the 2022 Conference on Empirical Methods in Natural Language Processing, Abu Dhabi, United Arab Emirates (2022)
11. Ghosh, S., Baker, D., Jurgens, D., Prabhakaran, V.: Detecting cross-geographic biases in toxicity modeling on social media. In: Proceedings of the Seventh Workshop on Noisy User-Generated Text, Punta Cana, the Dominican Republic (2021)
12. Goldfarb-Tarrant, S., Marchant, R., Sánchez, R.M., Pandya, M., Lopez, A.: Intrinsic bias metrics do not correlate with application bias. In: Proceedings of the 59th Annual Meeting of the Association for Computational Linguistics and the 11th International Joint Conference on Natural Language, Bangkok, Thailand (2021)

13. Goyal, T., Li, J.J., Durrett, G.: News summarization and evaluation in the era of GPT-3. arXiv preprint arXiv:2209.12356 (2023)
14. Jin, X., Barbieri, F., Kennedy, B., Davani, A.M., Neves, L., Ren, X.: On transferability of bias mitigation effects in language model fine-tuning. In: Proceedings of the Association for Computational Linguistics: NAACL 2021 (2021)
15. Kurita, K., Vyas, N., Pareek, A., Black, A.W., Tsvetkov, Y.: Measuring bias in contextualized word representations. In: Proceedings of the First Workshop on Gender Bias in Natural Language Processing, Florence, Italy (2019)
16. Li, Y., Zhang, G., Yang, B., Lin, C., Ragni, A., Wang, S., Fu, J.: HERB: measuring hierarchical regional bias in pre-trained language models. In: Proceedings of the 60th Annual Meeting of the Association for Computational Linguistics, Dublin, United Kingdom (2022)
17. Liu, R., Jia, C., Wei, J., Xu, G., Wang, L., Vosoughi, S.: Mitigating political bias in language models through reinforced calibration. In: Proceedings of the AAAI Conference on Artificial Intelligence (2021)
18. Liu, Y., Zhang, X.F., Wegsman, D., Beauchamp, N., Wang, L.: POLITICS: pretraining with same-story article comparison for ideology prediction and stance detection. In: Findings of the Association for Computational Linguistics: NAACL 2022, Washington, United States (2022)
19. Makazhanov, A., Rafiei, D.: Predicting political preference of twitter users. In: Proceedings of the 2013 IEEE/ACM International Conference on Advances in Social Networks Analysis and Mining, Ontario, Canada (2013)
20. Microsoft: Microsoft copilot is now generally available. Microsoft Bing Blogs (2023). https://blogs.bing.com/search/december-2023/Microsoft-Copilot-is-now-generally-available
21. Pichai, S., Hassabis, D.: Introducing Gemini: our largest and most capable AI model. Google The Keyword (2023). https://blog.google/technology/ai/google-gemini-ai
22. Preoţiuc-Pietro, D., Liu, Y., Hopkins, D., Ungar, L.: Beyond binary labels: political ideology prediction of Twitter users. In: Proceedings of the 55th Annual Meeting of the Association for Computational Linguistics, Vancouver, Canada (2017)
23. Shaikh, O., Zhang, H., Held, W., Bernstein, M., Yang, D.: On second thought, let's not think step by step! bias and toxicity in zero-shot reasoning. arXiv preprint arXiv:2212.08061 (2022)
24. Zhang, W., Feng, S., Chen, Z., Lei, Z., Li, J., Luo, M.: KCD: knowledge walks and textual cues enhanced political perspective detection in news media. In: Proceedings of the Association for Computational Linguistics: NAACL 2022, Washington, United States (2022)
25. Zhao, J., Wang, T., Yatskar, M., Ordonez, V., Chang, K.W.: Gender bias in coreference resolution: evaluation and debiasing methods. In: Proceedings of the Association for Computational Linguistics: NAACL 2018, Louisiana, Unites States (2018)

Fairness Analysis of Machine Learning-Based Code Reviewer Recommendation

Mohammad Mahdi Mohajer[1(✉)], Alvine Boaye Belle[1], Nima Shiri Harzevili[1], Junjie Wang[2], Hadi Hemmati[1], Song Wang[1], and Zhen Ming (Jack) Jiang[1]

[1] York University, Toronto, ON, Canada
{mmm98,nshiri,hemmati,wangsong}@yorku.ca, alvine.belle@lassonde.yorku.ca, zmjiang@cse.yorku.ca
[2] Institute of Software, Chinese Academy of Sciences, Beijing, China
junjie@iscas.ac.cn

Abstract. Ensuring the fairness of machine learning (ML) applications is critical to the reliability of modern artificial intelligence systems. Despite extensive study on this topic, the fairness of ML models in the software engineering (SE) domain has not yet been explored well. As a result, many ML-powered software systems, particularly those utilized in the software engineering community, continue to be prone to fairness issues. Taking one of the typical SE tasks, i.e., code reviewer recommendation, as a subject, this paper investigates the fairness of ML applications in the SE domain, specifically focusing on the code reviewer recommendation task. Our empirical study demonstrates that existing ML-based code reviewer recommendation systems exhibit unfairness and discriminating behaviors. Specifically, male reviewers get, on average, 7.25% more recommendations than female code reviewers compared to their distribution in the reviewer set. This paper also investigates why the studied ML-based code reviewer recommendation systems are unfair and provides solutions to mitigate the unfairness. For instance, such systems may recommend male reviewers at a significantly higher rate than female reviewers in a discriminatory manner. Our study further indicates that the existing mitigation methods can enhance fairness significantly in projects with a similar distribution of protected and privileged groups. Still, their effectiveness in improving fairness on imbalanced or skewed data is limited.

Keywords: Fairness · Machine Learning · Code Reviewer Recommendation

1 Introduction

Machine Learning (ML) approaches and models are increasingly being used in the development of modern software [49] to assist developers in different tasks, e.g., defect prediction [45,46], software bug triage [28], and code reviewer recommendation [13,37], etc. Meanwhile, the wide adoption of ML has given rise to new concerns and issues regarding the trustworthiness and ethicality of such systems, one of which is the issue of fairness [32,39].

Despite the fact that previous studies [7–11,21,25,41,44,51] have extensively examined the fairness of ML applications, while most of these studies mainly focus on general ML applications, little is known about the fairness of ML applications in software engineering domain, e.g., automated bug triage [28,52]. In this work, we take one of the typical SE tasks, i.e., code reviewer recommendation as a subject to explore the fairness of ML applications in SE domain. Specifically, code reviewer recommendation systems are widely used in modern software development to identify the most appropriate code reviewers for a code change. Recently, many ML-based code reviewer recommendation systems have been proposed. For instance, Patanamon et al. proposed RevFinder that used a similarity of previously reviewed file path to recommend an appropriate code-reviewer [43] and Pandya et al. [37] proposed CORMS, which leveraged similarity analysis and support vector machine (SVM) models to recommend reviewers. Although these examined code reviewer recommendation approaches can achieve good performance, none of the fairness characteristics (e.g., race, age, and gender) were considered when recommending reviewers. As a result, there may be bias or fairness issues in such systems that have not previously been investigated, which can potentially harm reviewers' activities. [9,39,41]. For example, in such systems, the final recommendation list may exhibit a need for more representation of female reviewers, as they might be recommended less frequently than their male counterparts in a biased manner.

To address the aforementioned concerns, in this paper, we look into the problem of assessing fairness issues in ML-based code reviewer recommendation systems. Specifically, we conduct an empirical study on two recent ML-based code reviewer recommendation systems, RevFinder [43] and CORMS [37], and we use the same dataset from CORMS [37] to build these systems and run our experiments. Note that, when exploring the fairness of ML-based code reviewer recommendation systems, we only consider the factor of gender. This is mainly because collecting data to identify sensitive factors such as age or race is difficult, as reviewers and code review platforms often do not disclose this information. Moreover, since obtaining non-binary gender information is difficult, and in line with previous fairness research [10,11,25,32,39] that used gender as the sensitive attribute, we are treating gender as a binary attribute in our analysis. Nevertheless, it's essential to emphasize that our study's scope is not confined to binary values and can be expanded to include non-binary genders if we acquire adequate data (details are provided in Sect. 3.2). Our experimental results show that both RevFinder and CORMS have unfair behavior in their recommendations. Specifically, they favor male reviewers over female reviewers. For example, we observe that in the Node.js project, male reviewers recommended by CORMS have approximately 85% more chance of being recommended for new code review requests, which is 16% more than the fair condition (details are in Sect. 4). We further explore the underlying factors that contribute to the unfairness of ML-based code reviewer recommendation systems, e.g., popularity bias, and whether the existing unfairness mitigation approaches [17,20,40,50] can help improve the fairness of these systems. Our experiment results show that the existing mitigation approaches can improve fairness, but not consistently across all projects. This study contributes to creating fairer ML-based code reviewer recommendation systems, reducing gender-based discrimination, and promoting societal equality and fairness. Those creating systems that engage with humans can apply the findings and methodology from our research to ensure their software products are equitable and contribute to equality among users. The methods used in our study also apply to other types of recommendation systems, such as team recommendation systems for collaborative software development [2]. As a summary, this paper makes the following contributions:

- We conduct an empirical study to investigate the fairness of two recent ML-based code reviewer recommendation systems.
- We analyze the underlying factors that influence the outcomes of code reviewer recommendation systems and demonstrate that the existing unfairness mitigation methods can be utilized to alleviate the unfairness in ML-based code reviewer recommendation systems.
- We show that the current mitigation approaches have limitations in terms of fairness improvement for projects with imbalanced or skewed data.
- We release the dataset and source code of our experiments to help other researchers replicate and extend our study[1].

2 Background and Related Work

2.1 Code Reviewer Recommendation System

A code reviewer recommendation system is a software application that supports software development teams in identifying the most appropriate code reviewers for a particular code change request by suggesting a list of the most qualified candidates to conduct the review request [16].

While the first code reviewer recommendation system already utilized machine learning techniques when it was introduced [22], earlier systems often relied on heuristic approaches [3,36], such as graph and search-based approaches. As an example, Ounti et al. [36] proposed RevRec, a recommendation system that uses a genetic algorithm to find an appropriate peer reviewer for a code change. As the field progressed, newer systems increasingly employed more machine learning methods [14,37,42,48] e.g., SVM (Support Vector Machines), collaborative filtering, and Naive Bayes, to improve their recommendations. These reviewer recommendation systems use different factors and features for determining the most qualified reviewer for a review request, such as file similarity, developers' expertise, social relations, developers' activeness, etc. [16].

---

[1] https://doi.org/10.5281/zenodo.11054911.

In this work, we select two state-of-the-art ML-based code reviewer recommendation systems, i.e., RevFinder [43] and CORMS [37], as our research subjects to explore their fairness (details are in Sect. 3.3). These code reviewer recommendation systems have been shown to outperform their prior baselines and have been found effective in recommending code reviewers.

2.2 Fairness Analysis in Machine Learning Application

In machine learning applications, there are two common types of fairness [32,39]: i.e., 1) Group Fairness, which ensures that different groups of people, including protected groups and privileged groups, are treated similarly and fairly. For example, in cases where gender is not a deciding factor, the female group should be treated similarly to the other groups (e.g., the male group) [32,39] and 2) Individual Fairness which ensures that individuals that are similar based on a criterion should be treated fairly and similarly [1,32,39]. For example, regardless of demographic background, each applicant in the employment process should be treated equitably. In this study, we conduct our analysis based on the group fairness definition. Rather than focusing on individual cases, group fairness analysis evaluates the influence of machine learning models on distinct groups of people.

2.3 Unfairness in Recommendation Systems

In this work, we focus on the fairness of recommendation systems. The concepts and definitions of fairness analysis in recommendation systems and general ML applications slightly differ [47]. For example, in previous studies [25,32,39], since all approaches target classification problems, the concept of fairness thoroughly depends on the predictions of the target attribute and its relation to the protected group. On the contrary, the concept of fairness in recommendation systems can be discussed from several points of view, e.g., the fairness of each of the recommended items (item-based fairness) and the fairness of the exposure and quality that each user experiences from the recommended items (user-based fairness) [47]. Also, in recommendation systems, not all of the biases are considered as unfairness, e.g., popularity bias, position bias, and conformity bias [12,47]. The fairness of recommendation systems can be categorized into two groups [47]:

- Process fairness: This means ensuring that the process used to produce recommendations is fair and unbiased to all users, regardless of their sensitive attributes.
- Outcome fairness: This means ensuring that the system's outcomes are distributed fairly and proportionately among various groups of people. This means that recommendations should neither favor nor discriminate against any particular group based on their sensitive attributes.

In this study, we focus on investigating **outcome fairness** in ML-powered code reviewer recommendation systems, specifically we examine the **item-based**

fairness through **group fairness** analysis. In particular, the items being recommended in our case are code reviewers. Therefore, our research focuses on assessing whether the final list of recommendations upholds fairness with regards to these recommended code reviewers.

2.4 Unfairness Mitigation Techniques

To mitigate the unfairness in ML applications, many unfairness mitigation mechanisms have been proposed [32,39], which can be categorized into three major types, i.e., pre-processing strategies [17,40] (by modifying training data before it is utilized for training), in-processing approaches [5,27] (by altering the machine-learning algorithm to increase fairness), post-processing techniques [23,34] (by updating output scores and predictions of the machine learning models). In this work, we focus on the "post-processing" category of fairness mitigation methods and exclude both "in-processing" and "pre-processing" mitigation approaches. "in-processing" approaches require non-trivial changes to the code reviewer recommendation systems, which are not generalizable. Additionally, the majority of "pre-processing" approaches are unsuitable for the recommendation tasks employed in our study subjects, given the inherent characteristics of our data, thus not suitable for fairness study in recommendation systems [17,40]. In many "pre-processing" methods, unfairness is often identified by analyzing proxy attributes, which are features correlated to sensitive attributes [25,32,39]. These methods heavily rely on numerical features. However, in the code reviewer recommendation systems we studied, the features are not numerical. Additionally, vector embedding as a way to calculate the score and rank the code reviewers is not used among both recommendation systems, as only CORMS uses this approach partially in its hybrid workflow [37]. Instead, using string-matching methods, RevFinder and CORMS determine the reviewers' scores based on the similarity between the file paths used in previous reviews [37,43]. This limited use of vector embedding and the non-numerical nature of the features in our studied systems pose significant challenges unique to our subjects. As a result, many "pre-processing" techniques are not applicable in this specific scenario, highlighting the need to focus more on "post-processing" approaches.

3 Empirical Study Setup

3.1 Research Questions

In this study, we are going to answer the following three research questions (RQs):

RQ1 (Existence of Fairness): Is there any unfairness in the ML-based code reviewer recommendation systems?

RQ2 (Root Cause for Unfairness): What is the root cause for unfairness in the code reviewer recommendation systems?

RQ3 (Effectiveness of Existing Unfairness Mitigation Techniques): Do existing unfairness mitigation approaches work for ML-based code reviewer recommendation systems?

3.2 Data Collection

For our analysis, we need datasets that include human-related information of reviewers, such as their gender, which is our desired sensitive attribute. However, existing code reviewer recommendation datasets from previous studies [37,43, 47] do not include that critical information. To collect the gender information of reviewers, in this work, we propose heuristic methods to infer a reviewer's gender information from their names and other publicly available information online (e.g., homepage, GitHub account information, and LinkedIn profile). Our experiment is conducted on the same dataset as the previous study [37], which includes code review requests from 34 open-source projects. These code review requests are collected from code review platforms like Gerrit and GitHub that are available to the public. As mentioned before, these code review systems do not keep reviewers' human-related information, such as gender, and we cannot directly obtain the genders of the reviewers from the datasets.

For each project in our dataset, we first get reviewers' names through the user ID provided by the code review platform. Then we use the following steps to infer a reviewer's demographic gender.

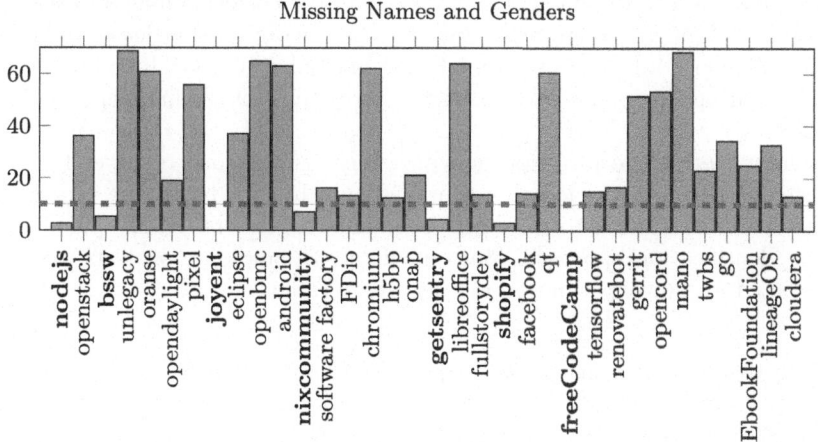

Fig. 1. The percentages of missing names and genders ("unknown") for each project examined in our study. We select projects with at most 10% missing names and genders, which is any project whose bar is beneath the red dashed line. (Color figure online)

We first remove projects that have a high percentage of reviewers with missing names. If the field for a reviewer's name is null or blank, we consider this as not having a name mainly because the reviewer did not specify a name on his/her profile. Also, reviewers may have nicknames instead of their real names on their profiles. We consider all these records "unknown" since we cannot infer the gender from them. To distinguish nicknames from real names, we use the following heuristic, i.e., if a name contains any number, symbol, or sign, we consider that a nickname; e.g., in the nixcommunity project, there was a reviewer with the name "jD91mZM2", which has been removed from the data. We discard projects with reviewers who have more than 10% "unknown" names to ensure the quality of our experiment data. The missing rates are demonstrated in Fig. 1. As a result, we selected seven out of 34 projects. In the seven projects examined, there were at most four reviewers who had nicknames on their profiles.

Second, for the selected seven projects, we manually check each reviewer's information through online resources, e.g., personal and institutional homepages, GitHub accounts, and LinkedIn profiles. Some of the reviewers have links to their social media accounts on their GitHub profiles, so we can access their information directly. For the reviewers who do not provide social connections (20% of our reviewer set), we search their full name on the internet to find their social media accounts and get their gender information. During the process, we discard names that point to indistinguishable users (e.g., people who have the same name and similar profiles on social media). We look for gender information in their specified pronouns in their profiles, and their online content, including the pronouns and genders the reviewers themselves or others used to describe them. In this manual analysis, we checked 355 reviewers' information on the internet. These reviewers may possess several reviews and contributions in our dataset, employed for training the models, and the corresponding statistics are displayed in Table 1. According to our analysis, we obtained at least 90% of the reviewers' gender information through this manual analysis. Three authors are involved during this process to ensure the correctness of the manually analyzed results.

Finally, we remove projects for which there is only one reviewer from the protected group, i.e., the female reviewer group. In each remaining project, we exclude records relating to reviewers of unknown genders. After applying our gender identification approach, four out of the 34 candidate projects from [37] are selected for our experiments, details are in Table 1.

Table 1. Details of the four selected projects. The columns "Missing Genders", "Total Ex.", "F. Ratio", "M#", and "F#", are the percentage of missing genders, the total number of examples, the ratio of female reviewers, the number of female reviewers, and the number of male reviewers, respectively.

Project	Missing Genders	Total Ex.	F.Ratio	F#	M#
nodejs	2.7%	110	0.13	5	28
bssw	5.2%	213	0.67	9	9
getsentry	4.1%	775	0.08	6	64
shopify	2.8%	565	0.06	17	148

3.3 Subjects of Study

As mentioned in Sect. 2.1, We use two recent existing ML-based code reviewer recommendation systems as the research subjects, i.e., CORMS [37] and RevFinder [43]. RevFinder recommends code reviewers based on a machine learning-based ranking algorithm that learns the scores of different candidates for a given review request based on the similarities in the file locations involved in past code reviews from the dataset. By evaluating the records in the dataset and propagating the scores of each reviewer involved in review requests with similar file path locations, RevFinder provides a list of unique reviewers and their scores for the given dataset. On the other hand, CORMS is a hybrid code reviewer recommendation system that uses the same similarity model as RevFinder (with additional features) and employs an SVM model that learns from each review subject in the training set. Finally, appropriate reviewers are chosen based on their computed scores and associated ranks corresponding to their scores in the final recommendation list.

Although these two code reviewer recommendation approaches that we have examined can achieve good performance in terms of accuracy of the reviewer recommendation task, none of the fairness characteristics, e.g., race, age, and gender, were considered when recommending reviewers by using these approaches. In this study, the female reviewer group is considered the protected group. Furthermore, we ensure the validity of our findings by replicating the configurations of the selected two code reviewer recommendation systems as specified in their respective publications [37,43].

It is worth noting that we are selecting the mentioned subjects because they are suitable for datasets that either contain human-related information or support indirectly adding human-related information to them to facilitate our analysis. Although there were also other different code reviewer recommendation systems, they were either trained on different datasets that are incompatible for fairness analysis or their architecture simply does not comply with our dataset.

3.4 Evaluation Measures

Existing studies [19,29] revealed that improving fairness usually comes at a cost in terms of performance measures such as model accuracy. As a result, in order to demonstrate that an unfairness mitigation strategy is useful to deploy, most studies in fairness analysis will include a performance measure before and after applying the unfairness mitigation technique [15,25,39]. This trade-off can be balanced through different approaches, but it also relies on the context and domain of the application and the extent to which we can sacrifice accuracy for fairness [4,15,19,24,29,33]. It is important to clarify that the objective of our study is to evaluate the fairness of code reviewer recommendation systems, rather than focusing on their performance. Performance measures are solely utilized to assess the influence of unfairness mitigation strategies on the recommendation outcomes, both before and after implementing these strategies. In this work, we follow existing studies [25,39] and use the average of all measure values for each record in our dataset to represent the overall performance.

Fairness Measures. To evaluate the fairness of recommendation systems, we use two measures that rely on the top-K results and one measure that is independent of the top-K results [20,47]. Similar to existing works [37,43] that conducted their experiments in a specific setting, we limit the values of K to 4, 6, and 10.

$Skew_{S_i}@K$: The skew of the ranked list of top-K candidates for a certain value S_i of the sensitive attribute is:

$$Skew_{S_i}@K(C) = \ln(\frac{P_{C^K,S_i}}{P_{D,S_i}}) \tag{1}$$

where C is the ranked list of candidates, C^K is the top-K candidates from C, P_{C^K,S_i} is the proportion of candidates having the sensitive attribute value S_i in the top-K results, and P_{D,S_i} is the desired proportion of candidates with the sensitive attribute value S_i in the given dataset.

Statistical Parity Difference For top-K results ($SPD@K$): The statistical parity difference (SPD) is a well-known measure of fairness that is used in many articles about how fair machine learning is when it comes to classification tasks [25,39]. This measure is demonstrated in Eq. 2 as an example for the binary classification:

$$\left|P[\hat{Y}=1|S=1] - P[\hat{Y}=1|S\neq 1]\right| \leq \epsilon \tag{2}$$

Nevertheless, to use this measure for top-K results in recommendation systems such as code reviewer recommendation systems, we must change the calculation in Eq. 2. As a result, we introduce the $SPD@K$ measure, which is described in Eq. 3:

$$\left|P[\hat{Y} \in C^K|S=1] - P[\hat{Y} \in C^K|S \neq 1]\right| \leq \epsilon \tag{3}$$

where C^K is the ranked list of top-K candidates from the ranked list of candidates C as the result of the recommendation. In this measure, we also refer to ϵ as the expected SPD threshold. This threshold will be computed by calculating the absolute difference between the male and female ratios in the dataset, which is described in Eq. 4:

$$\epsilon = \left|\frac{\#Females}{\#Reviewers} - \frac{\#Males}{\#Reviewers}\right| \tag{4}$$

The reason that we calculate an expected value for ϵ as depicted in Eq. 4 is that we expect that the difference in recommendation rates for males and females should be similar to the disparity in ratios of these groups in the dataset. Although ϵ can be variable and should usually be identified by domain experts of the application in which the fairness analysis is being conducted [39], Eq. 4 is still a reasonable statistical estimation of the difference between the rates of recommendations for both privileged and unprivileged groups to be in a fair state.

Normalized Discounted Cumulative KL-divergence (NDKL): Eq. 5 describes the normalized discounted cumulative Kullback-Leiber (KL) divergence given a ranked list of the candidates C:

$$NDKL(C) = \frac{1}{Z} \sum_{i \in K_s} \frac{1}{\log_2(i+1)} d_{\mathrm{KL}}(D_{C^i} || D_d) \qquad (5)$$

In Eq. 5 $d_{\mathrm{KL}}(D_{C^i} || D_d) = \sum_j D_{C^i}(j) \ln \frac{D_{C^i}(j)}{D_d}$, $Z = \sum_{i=1}^{C} \frac{1}{\log_2(i+1)}$, and $K_s = \{4, 6, 10\}$ where D_{C^i} and D_d represent the proportion of the top i candidates in the ranked list of candidates C having the sensitive attribute j, respectively, and the desired proportion based on the dataset with the sensitive attribute value j.

Performance Measures. In this study, we adopt the identical performance metrics utilized in previous research papers discussing CORMS and RevFinder [37,43], i.e., Top-K Accuracy and Mean Reciprocal Rank (MRR). This enables us to cross-compare and guarantee accurate replications of both works and to ensure a fair assessment before and after applying bias mitigation strategies. In our scenario, we use $MRR@K$ to focus on the top-K recommendations. This means that we only consider the top-K candidates in the original calculations. Every candidate not on the top-K list has a reciprocal rank of zero. The rest of the calculations remain the same.

3.5 Selected Unfairness Mitigation Approaches

Researchers have proposed several unfairness mitigation strategies for recommendation systems [6,20,26,35,38,47,50], but not all of them are applicable to our case due to different views on fairness [47] (more details in Sect. 2.3) and limitations around different techniques such as "in-processing" and "pre-processing" approaches (more details in Sect. 2.4). Also, due to the inherent differences in the fairness of classification and recommendation tasks (e.g., techniques used for classification do not support top-K results), we cannot employ those mitigation techniques for classification tasks in our study [47]. Moreover, each recommendation system can have a distinct and different architecture, and only some mitigation techniques apply to that type of architecture (e.g., reinforcement learning-based approaches may not be suitable for many recommendation systems) [47]. Also, although there were various "post-processing" mitigation approaches in the literature, not all could be easily adapted and applied to our study subjects. For example, the re-ranking approaches proposed by Liu et al. [31] and Naghiaei et al. [35] look at the fairness of recommendation from a multi-sided perspective. In contrast, in our study, we only focus on item-based fairness, which is the fairness of the reviewers recommended for each review request (more details in Sect. 2.3).

Thus, in this work, we select two applicable approaches from the "post-processing" category of fairness mitigation methods (see Sect. 2.4) for reviewer recommendation systems [47]. The details of these two mitigation approaches are as follows.

DetGreedy Algorithm. Geyik et al. [20] developed this algorithm for fairness-aware recommendation in LinkedIn Talent Search recommendation systems. This algorithm works as follows. Given a top-K list, there are two requirements to satisfy the fairness condition:

a. Min: $\forall K < |C| \wedge \forall s_i \in A, count_K(S_i) \geq \lfloor P_{D,S_i} \cdot K \rfloor$
b. Max: $\forall K < |C| \wedge \forall s_i \in A, count_K(S_i) \leq \lceil P_{D,S_i} \cdot K \rceil$

where A is the set of attribute values, C is the list of candidates, P_{D,S_i} is the desired proportion of candidates with the attribute value S_i, and $count_k(S_i)$ is the number of candidates with the attribute value S_i in the top-K results. If some candidates are close to not meeting the minimum requirement, select the one with the highest score from that group. If all candidates meet the minimum requirement, choose the one with the highest score among those who have not yet reached their maximum requirements.

DetRelaxed. To improve DetGreedy, Geyik et al. [20] further proposed DetRelaxed. While DetGreedy aims to include as many high-scoring candidates as possible in the ranked list, it may not be effective in various scenarios, according to the authors [20]. The DetRelaxed algorithm was proposed to consider all candidates who satisfy the minimum requirement and minimize the term $\left\lceil \frac{\lceil P_{D,S_i} \cdot K \rceil}{P_{D,S_i}} \right\rceil$ to select the candidate with the highest score for the next position.

The formulas and details mentioned for both approaches are based on Geyik et al.'s study [20], which you can refer to for more information. According to this research study [20], these approaches resulted in a huge improvement in fairness at the production stage. Hence, we select these approaches to assess their effectiveness with our subjects.

4 Results and Analysis

4.1 RQ1: Existence of Fairness

Approach: To answer this RQ, we first build RevFinder and CORMS on the training data selected from our experimental dataset (details are in Sect. 3.2). When training each model, following existing studies [37,43], we divide the dataset into two sections, with 80% for training and the remaining 20% for testing, chronologically. Then, we use the measures mentioned in Sect. 3.4 to evaluate the fairness of the recommendations generated by these code reviewer recommendation systems based on the testing data.

Result: Table 2 presents the findings of our experiments, where we analyze all the evaluation measures for each project across three different scenarios, i.e., original (i.e., results obtained without any mitigation approaches), DG (i.e., outcomes obtained after using DetGreedy), and DR (i.e., results obtained after using DetRelaxed). Also, it presents the SPD threshold for each project in the dataset. As we can see from column "Original" in the table, $Skew@K$ has negative values under both CORMS and RevFinder on the four projects with different K values, e.g., BSSW, GetSentry, Node.js, and Shopify, which have negative $Skew@K$ values, i.e., -0.19, -0.01, -0.73, and -0.90 under CORMS when recommending top 10 reviewers. For $SPD@K$, as we can see on most projects, the values of $SPD@K$ are above the specified threshold values which indicates that the disparity between the percentages of males and females being recommended in BSSW, GetSentry, Node.js, and Shopify projects is 15%, 3%, 3%, and 8%, respectively. Overall, considering the different $SPD@K$ metric variations and their corresponding expected SPD threshold, male reviewers get an average of 7.25% more recommendations than female code reviewers compared to their distribution in the reviewer set. This calculation involves averaging across all the mentioned variations. Results from $Skew@K$ and $SPD@K$ indicate there are unfairness issues for each of the four experimental projects under both CORMS and RevFinder.

Table 2. Summary of experiment results. The results that are considered unfair recommendations based on the $SPD@K$ and $Skew@K$ measures are highlighted in ● and ●, respectively.

Top-K	Subjects	Measures	BSSW			GetSentry			Node.js			Shopify		
			Original	DG	DR	Original	DG	DR	Original	DG	DR	Original	DG	DR
Top-4	CORMS	TopK-ACC	79%	79%	79%	43%	43%	37%	41%	41%	41%	25%	25%	30%
		MRR@K	0.54	0.54	0.54	0.23	0.23	0.21	0.26	0.26	0.27	0.19	0.19	0.21
		SPD@K	0	0	0	0.93	0.93	1	0.85	0.85	1	0.80	0.87	1
		Skew@K	0.01	0.01	0.01	−1.82	−1.82	−2.25	−1.79	−1.79	−2.7	−1.41	−1.50	−2.35
	RevFinder	TopK-ACC	71%	73%	73%	43%	43%	37%	50%	50%	45%	25%	25%	24%
		MRR@K	0.5	0.5	0.5	0.25	0.25	0.22	0.32	0.32	0.31	0.15	0.15	0.14
		SPD@K	0.09	0	0	0.90	0.88	1	0.52	0.56	1	0.97	0.96	1
		Skew@K	−0.001	0.01	0.01	−1.48	−1.48	−2.12	0.15	0.09	−2.71	−2.03	−1.94	−2.17
Top-6	CORMS	TopK-ACC	84%	87%	87%	44%	44%	38%	52%	52%	47%	34%	36%	37%
		MRR@K	0.55	0.56	0.56	0.24	0.24	0.21	0.29	0.29	0.28	0.21	0.21	0.22
		SPD@K	0.31	0	0	0.87	0.87	1	0.86	0.86	0.66	0.80	0.87	1
		Skew@K	−0.35	0.01	0.01	−1.20	−1.20	−2.25	−1.56	−1.56	0.12	−1.14	−1.28	−2.35
	RevFinder	TopK-ACC	88%	83%	83%	49%	49%	46%	54%	54%	54%	36%	36%	37%
		MRR@K	0.53	0.52	0.52	0.26	0.26	0.24	0.33	0.33	0.33	0.17	0.17	0.17
		SPD@K	0.13	0	0	0.81	0.80	1	0.60	0.69	0.66	0.97	0.96	1
		Skew@K	−0.14	0.01	0.01	−0.53	−0.58	−2.12	−0.1	0.15	−1.97	−1.87	−2.17	
Top-10	CORMS	TopK-ACC	94%	100%	100%	45%	46%	45%	58%	58%	58%	42%	43%	46%
		MRR@K	0.57	0.57	0.57	0.24	0.24	0.24	0.29	0.29	0.29	0.22	0.22	0.22
		SPD@K	0.2	0	0	0.79	0.82	0.8	0.82	0.78	0.8	0.77	0.73	0.8
		Skew@K	−0.19	0.01	0.01	−0.01	−0.1	0.14	−0.73	−0.31	−0.35	−0.90	0.26	0.04
	RevFinder	TopK-ACC	88%	92%	92%	62%	62%	55%	68%	68%	68%	44%	44%	43%
		MRR@K	0.53	0.53	0.53	0.28	0.28	0.25	0.35	0.35	0.35	0.18	0.18	0.17
		SPD@K	0.17	0	0	0.81	0.82	1	0.68	0.68	0.8	0.96	0.96	1
		Skew@K	−0.19	0.01	0.01	−0.03	−0.16	−2.12	0.06	0.06	−0.32	−1.83	−1.77	−2.17
	CORMS	NDKL	0.04	0.01	0.01	0.08	0.08	0.08	0.11	0.10	0.08	0.14	0.08	0.09
	RevFinder	NDKL	0.04	0.01	0.01	0.07	0.07	0.09	0.06	0.06	0.08	0.09	0.09	0.10
	SPD Threshold		0			0.82			0.69			0.79		

Furthermore, we analyze the normalized discounted KL divergence measure (NDKL), which is shown in Table 2. Our experiments indicate that the NDKL measure yielded positive values for all projects, suggesting that the outcomes may be biased towards a particular value of the sensitive attribute.

> **Answer to RQ1:** In the examined projects, male reviewers get an average of 7.25% more recommendations than female code reviewers, considering their distribution in the recommendation list under both CORMS and RevFinder. Our experiment results suggest that the two ML-based code reviewer recommendation systems studied exhibit bias towards gender.

4.2 RQ2: Root Cause for Unfairness

Approach: To answer this question, we first conduct an exclusive analysis of current fairness studies in the literature to collect all the possible factors that have been examined to be effective in determining the fairness of ML applications [12,32,39,47,53], especially recommendation systems. Three factors were collected: (1) imbalanced or skewed data, (2) popularity bias, and (3) algorithmic objectives.

Note that we exclude the factor of algorithmic objectives since it requires us to examine the code reviewer recommendation architectures, which is out of the scope of this paper. As a result, we employ the factors of imbalanced or skewed data and popularity bias to explore the possible root causes of code reviewer recommendation systems. Imbalanced or skewed data can lead to unfairness because models trained on such data have a strong probability of learning behavior towards over-represented groups, eventually becoming overfitted to them [12,47]. Popularity bias and unfairness also have a strong connection with each other [12,53]. The "long-tail effect" occurs when recommendation systems favor popular items over less popular ones [18,30], which leads to discrimination against the less popular items. If the less popular items are generally from the protected group, popularity bias will turn into unfairness.

Result: The following are the primary factors responsible for the unfairness and disparities between actual and expected distributions of the protected group in the outputs of the code reviewer recommendation system:

Imbalanced or Skewed Data: Our analysis indicates that the imbalanced representation of male and female reviewers in some projects is one of the reasons behind the unfair outcomes of code reviewer recommendation systems. Table 1 shows that, apart from the BSSW project, which has an equal number of female and male reviewers, the number of male reviewers is higher than that of female reviewers in all other projects (males are approximately 8 times more than females), which leads to skewed data. The BSSW project has a record of females accounting for 67% of the total, while in the Node.js, GetSentry, and Shopify projects, this percentage is 13%, 8%, and 6%, respectively. Consequently, Table 2 reveals that the results of the $SPD@K$ measure for the BSSW project are substantially lower than those of other projects, suggesting a fairer outcome. The same pattern is observed for the $Skew@K$ measure in the BSSW project, as other projects exhibit more negative values for this measure, indicating larger discrepancies between the current and fair conditions.

Popularity Bias: In the projects examined, bias was found to be more prevalent in projects where male reviewers were more popular than female reviewers. For instance, in Shopify and Node.js, the first 14% and 15% of popular reviewers were all male, respectively. This led to unfairness in the CORMS and RevFinder recommendation systems, which learned and incorporated this preference for male reviewers into their decision-making processes. In contrast, in the BSSW project, the first two popular reviewers were female, resulting in fairness measures like $Skew@K$ and $SPD@K$ being closer to fair values, such as $Skew@K$ being closer to zero.

> **Answer to RQ2:** We confirm that popularity bias and imbalanced or skewed data are two factors that can affect code reviewer recommendation systems, both of which can lead to unfairness. Projects that do not have these issues (e.g., BSSW) result in values in fairness measures that are closer to a fair state, in contrast to projects that do suffer from these problems.

4.3 RQ3: Effectiveness of Existing Unfairness Mitigation Techniques

Approach: In this RQ, we examine the selected unfairness mitigation approaches (i.e., DetGreedy and DetRelaxed) in Sect. 3.5 to see if they could improve the fairness of code reviewer recommendation systems. Furthermore, because applying an unfairness mitigation technique has been shown to have a trade-off with performance measures [15,29], we should also guarantee that applying these mechanisms does not adversely affect performance measures. As a result, we compare performance measures before and after using unfairness mitigation techniques.

Result: The fairness measures after applying these two mitigation approaches, i.e., DetGreedy and DetRelaxed, for each project, are shown in Table 2.

As we can see from the table, both DetGreedy and DetRelaxed mitigation techniques can improve fairness, but not across all projects. The bolded values on this table indicate fairness improvements compared to original settings. With the use of these approaches, the BSSW project saw a significant fairness improvement of 100%. Also, in the BSSW project, RevFinder's top-K accuracy decreased by 5% solely in the top-6 scenario. While performance measures were not adversely impacted (only a 1.75% decrease on average on all projects), the fairness enhancement was not as noticeable in projects with an imbalanced distribution of male and female reviewers (e.g., Node.js, GetSentry, and Shopify). Thus, to mitigate unfairness in code reviewer recommendation systems, we should select a mitigation technique that aligns with the dataset's characteristics or performs independently of those characteristics.

> **Answer to RQ3:** DetGreedy and DetRelaxed mitigation approaches can improve fairness while maintaining performance, but not consistently across all projects.

5 Conclusion

This paper represents a novel investigation into the fairness issue of machine learning-based code reviewer recommendation systems. Specifically, two recent existing systems (CORMS and RevFinder) and code review data from four open-source projects were used to conduct the fairness analysis. Our empirical study demonstrates that current ML-based code reviewer recommendation techniques exhibit unfairness and discriminating behaviors. This paper also discusses the reasons why the studied ML-based code reviewer recommendation systems are unfair and provides solutions to mitigate the unfairness.

References

1. How do fairness definitions fare? examining public attitudes towards algorithmic definitions of fairness. In: AIES 2019, pp. 99–106 (2019)
2. Tuarob, S., Assavakamhaenghan, N., Tanaphantaruk, W., Suwanworaboon, P., Hassan, S.U., Choetkiertikul, M.: Automatic team recommendation for collaborative software development. Empir. Softw. Eng. **26**, 1–53 (2021)
3. Sülün, E., Tüzün, E., Doğrusöz, U.: RSTrace+: reviewer suggestion using software artifact traceability graphs. Inf. Softw. Technol. **130**, 106455 (2021)
4. Bechavod, Y., Ligett, K.: Penalizing unfairness in binary classification. arXiv preprint arXiv:1707.00044 (2017)
5. Beutel, A., et al.: Fairness in recommendation ranking through pairwise comparisons. In: SIGKDD, KDD 2019, pp. 2212–2220 (2019)
6. Biega, A.J., Gummadi, K.P., Weikum, G.: Equity of attention: amortizing individual fairness in rankings. In: 41st International ACM SIGIR Conference on Research and Development in Information Retrieval, SIGIR 2018, vol. 18, pp. 405–414 (2018). https://doi.org/10.1145/3209978.3210063. https://dl.acm.org/doi/10.1145/3209978.3210063
7. Biswas, S., Rajan, H.: Do the machine learning models on a crowd sourced platform exhibit bias? An empirical study on model fairness. In: ESEC/FSE 2020, pp. 642–653 (2020)
8. Biswas, S., Rajan, H.: Fair preprocessing: towards understanding compositional fairness of data transformers in machine learning pipeline. In: ESEC/FSE 2021, vol. 21, pp. 981–993 (2021)
9. Brun, Y., Meliou, A.: Software fairness. In: ESEC/FSE, pp. 754–759 (2018)
10. Chakraborty, J., Majumder, S., Menzies, T.: Bias in machine learning software: Why? how? what to do? In: ESEC/FSE 2021, pp. 429–440 (2021)
11. Chakraborty, J., Majumder, S., Yu, Z., Menzies, T.: Fairway: a way to build fair ml software, pp. 654–665 (2020)
12. Chen, J., et al.: Bias and debias in recommender system: a survey and future directions. ACM Trans. Inf. Syst. **41**, 67 (2023)

13. Chouchen, M., Ouni, A., Mkaouer, M.W., Kula, R.G., Inoue, K.: WhoReview: a multi-objective search-based approach for code reviewers recommendation in modern code review. Appl. Soft Comput. **100**, 106908 (2021)
14. Chueshev, A., Lawall, J., Bendraou, R., Ziadi, T.: Expanding the number of reviewers in open-source projects by recommending appropriate developers. In: ICSME 2020, pp. 499–510 (2020)
15. Corbett-Davies, S., Pierson, E., Feller, A., Goel, S., Huq, A.: Algorithmic decision making and the cost of fairness. In: KDD 2017, pp. 797–806. Association for Computing Machinery (2017)
16. Davila, N., Nunes, I.: A systematic literature review and taxonomy of modern code review. J. Syst. Softw. **177**, 110951 (2021)
17. Ekstrand, M.D., et al.: All the cool kids, how do they fit in?: Popularity and demographic biases in recommender evaluation and effectiveness. In: Friedler, S.A., Wilson, C. (eds.) Proceedings of Machine Learning Research, vol. 81, pp. 172–186. PMLR, 23–24 February 2018
18. Ferraro, A.: Music cold-start and long-tail recommendation: bias in deep representations. In: RecSys 2019, pp. 586–590 (2019)
19. Friedler, S.A., Scheidegger, C., Venkatasubramanian, S., Choudhary, S., Hamilton, E.P., Roth, D.: A comparative study of fairness-enhancing interventions in machine learning. In: Proceedings of the Conference on Fairness, Accountability, and Transparency, FAT* 2019, pp. 329–338. Association for Computing Machinery, New York (2019). https://doi.org/10.1145/3287560.3287589
20. Geyik, S.C., Ambler, S., Kenthapadi, K.: Fairness-aware ranking in search and recommendation systems with application to linkedin talent search. In: KDD 2019, pp. 2221–2231 (2019)
21. Hort, M., Zhang, J.M., Sarro, F., Harman, M.: Fairea: a model behaviour mutation approach to benchmarking bias mitigation methods. In: ESEC/FSE 2021, pp. 994–1006 (2021)
22. Jeong, G., Kim, S., Zimmermann, T., Yi, K.: Improving code review by predicting reviewers and acceptance of patches. In: Research on Software Analysis for Error-free Computing Center Tech-Memo (ROSAEC MEMO 2009-006), pp. 1–18 (2009)
23. Kaya, M., Bridge, D., Tintarev, N.: Ensuring fairness in group recommendations by rank-sensitive balancing of relevance. In: RecSys 2020, pp. 101–110 (2020)
24. Kleinberg, J.: Inherent trade-offs in algorithmic fairness. SIGMETRICS Perform. Eval. Rev. **46**(1), 40 (2018). https://doi.org/10.1145/3292040.3219634
25. Li, Y., et al.: Training data debugging for the fairness of machine learning software. In: ICSE 20222, pp. 2215–2227. Association for Computing Machinery (2022)
26. Li, Y., Chen, H., Fu, Z., Ge, Y., Zhang, Y.: User-oriented fairness in recommendation. In: The Web Conference 2021 - Proceedings of the World Wide Web Conference, WWW 2021, pp. 624–632 (2021). https://doi.org/10.1145/3442381.3449866. https://dl.acm.org/doi/10.1145/3442381.3449866
27. Li, Y., Chen, H., Xu, S., Ge, Y., Zhang, Y.: Towards personalized fairness based on causal notion. In: SIGIR 2021, pp. 1054–1063 (2021)
28. Li, Z., Zhong, H.: Revisiting textual feature of bug-triage approach. In: ASE 2021, pp. 1183–1185 (2021)
29. Lipton, Z.C., Chouldechova, A., McAuley, J.: Does mitigating ML's impact disparity require treatment disparity? In: Proceedings of the 32nd International Conference on Neural Information Processing Systems, NIPS 2018, pp. 8136–8146. Curran Associates Inc., Red Hook (2018)
30. Liu, S., Zheng, Y.: Long-tail session-based recommendation. In: RecSys 2020, pp. 509–514 (2020)

31. Liu, W., Guo, J., Sonboli, N., Burke, R., Zhang, S.: Personalized fairness-aware re-ranking for microlending. In: Proceedings of the 13th ACM Conference on Recommender Systems, RecSys 2019, pp. 467–471. Association for Computing Machinery, New York (2019). https://doi.org/10.1145/3298689.3347016
32. Mehrabi, N., Morstatter, F., Saxena, N., Lerman, K., Galstyan, A.: A survey on bias and fairness in machine learning. ACM Comput. Surv. (CSUR) **54**, 1–35 (2021)
33. Menon, A.K., Williamson, R.C.: The cost of fairness in binary classification. In: Friedler, S.A., Wilson, C. (eds.) Proceedings of the 1st Conference on Fairness, Accountability and Transparency. Proceedings of Machine Learning Research, vol. 81, pp. 107–118. PMLR, 23–24 February 2018. https://proceedings.mlr.press/v81/menon18a.html
34. Morik, M., Singh, A., Hong, J., Joachims, T.: Controlling fairness and bias in dynamic learning-to-rank. In: SIGIR 2020, pp. 429–438 (2020)
35. Naghiaei, M., Rahmani, H.A., Deldjoo, Y.: CPFair: personalized consumer and producer fairness re-ranking for recommender systems. In: Proceedings of the 45th International ACM SIGIR Conference on Research and Development in Information Retrieval, SIGIR 2022, pp. 770–779. Association for Computing Machinery, New York (2022). https://doi.org/10.1145/3477495.3531959
36. Ouni, A., Kula, R.G., Inoue, K.: Search-based peer reviewers recommendation in modern code review. In: ICSME 2016, pp. 367–377 (2016)
37. Pandya, P., Tiwari, S.: CORMS: a GitHub and Gerrit based hybrid code reviewer recommendation approach for modern code review, pp. 546–557. Association for Computing Machinery (ACM) (2022)
38. Patro, G.K., Biswas, A., Ganguly, N., Gummadi, K.P., Chakraborty, A.: FairRec: two-sided fairness for personalized recommendations in two-sided platforms. In: Proceedings of The Web Conference 2020, WWW 2020, pp. 1194–1204. Association for Computing Machinery, New York (2020). https://doi.org/10.1145/3366423.3380196
39. Pessach, D., Shmueli, E.: A review on fairness in machine learning. ACM Comput. Surv. **55**, 1–44 (2023). https://doi.org/10.1145/3494672
40. Rastegarpanah, B., Gummadi, K.P., Crovella, M.: Fighting fire with fire: using antidote data to improve polarization and fairness of recommender systems. In: WSDM 2019, pp. 231–239 (2019)
41. Soremekun, E., Papadakis, M., Cordy, M., Traon, Y.L.: Software fairness: an analysis and survey (2022)
42. Strand, A., Gunnarson, M., Britto, R., Usman, M.: Using a context-aware approach to recommend code reviewers: findings from an industrial case study. In: ICSE-SEIP 2020, pp. 1–10 (2020)
43. Thongtanunam, P., Tantithamthavorn, C., Kula, R.G., Yoshida, N., Iida, H., Matsumoto, K.I.: Who should review my code? A file location-based code-reviewer recommendation approach for modern code review. In: SANER 2015, pp. 141–150 (2015)
44. Tizpaz-Niari, S., Kumar, A., Tan, G., Trivedi, A.: Fairness-aware configuration of machine learning libraries. In: ICSE 2022, pp. 909–920 (2022)
45. Wang, S., Liu, T., Nam, J., Tan, L.: Deep semantic feature learning for software defect prediction. IEEE Trans. Software Eng. **46**(12), 1267–1293 (2020)
46. Wang, S., Liu, T., Tan, L.: Automatically learning semantic features for defect prediction. In: ICSE 2016, pp. 297–308 (2016)

47. Wang, Y., Ma, W., Zhang, M., Liu, Y., Ma, S.: A survey on the fairness of recommender systems. ACM Trans. Inf. Syst. **41**, 1–43 (2023). https://doi.org/10.1145/3547333
48. Xia, Z., Sun, H., Jiang, J., Wang, X., Liu, X.: A hybrid approach to code reviewer recommendation with collaborative filtering. In: MSR 2017, pp. 24–31 (2017)
49. Yang, Y., Xia, X., Lo, D., Grundy, J.: A survey on deep learning for software engineering. ACM Comput. Surv. **54**(10s) (2022). https://doi.org/10.1145/3505243
50. Zehlike, M., Bonchi, F., Castillo, C., Hajian, S., Megahed, M., Baeza-Yates, R.: FA*IR: a fair top-k ranking algorithm. In: International Conference on Information and Knowledge Management, Proceedings, pp. 1569–1578 (2017)
51. Zhang, J.M., Harman, M.: 'ignorance and prejudice' in software fairness. In: Proceedings - International Conference on Software Engineering, pp. 1436–1447 (2021). https://doi.org/10.1109/ICSE43902.2021.00129
52. Zhang, W.: Efficient bug triage for industrial environments. In: 2020 IEEE International Conference on Software Maintenance and Evolution (ICSME), pp. 727–735 (2020). https://doi.org/10.1109/ICSME46990.2020.00082
53. Zhu, Z., He, Y., Zhao, X., Zhang, Y., Wang, J., Caverlee, J.: Popularity-opportunity bias in collaborative filtering. In: WSDM 2021, pp. 85–93. Association for Computing Machinery, New York (2021)

Bias Reduction in Social Networks Through Agent-Based Simulations

Nathan Bartley(✉), Keith Burghardt, and Kristina Lerman

Information Sciences Institute, Marina Del Rey, CA 90292, USA
nbartley@usc.edu

Abstract. Online social networks use recommender systems to suggest relevant information to their users in the form of personalized timelines. Studying how these systems expose people to information at scale is difficult to do as one cannot assume each user is subject to the same timeline condition and building appropriate evaluation infrastructure is costly. We show that a simple agent-based model where users have fixed preferences affords us the ability to compare different recommender systems (and thus different personalized timelines) in their ability to skew users' perception of their network. Importantly, we show that a simple greedy algorithm that constructs a feed based on network properties reduces such perception biases comparable to a random feed. This underscores the influence network structure has in determining the effectiveness of recommender systems in the social network context and offers a tool for mitigating perception biases through algorithmic feed construction.

Keywords: Social Networks · Agent-based Models · Recommendations

Recommender systems are pervasive in online social media platforms and they span various functions including social link recommendations (e.g., "Who to Follow"), ad targeting (i.e., users are recommended for ad providers), geolocated news (e.g., Trending Topics), and content recommendation more broadly. While these recommender systems afford users the ability to sift through incredible amounts of information online, they have become the objects of study and critique for their plausible yet not well understood role in amplifying information [15,21].

To tease out the impact of the recommender systems, it is important not to overlook the role users play in their interactions with them. Recent work has explored user preferences in agent-based models on YouTube in regards to their primary video recommender system: however an important limitation in this line of work is the lack of comparison of different systems and different kinds of feeds, like those that appear in online social networks like X and Facebook [7,22]. There is a vein of work on X and Facebook that does consider user interactions as a factor in the differences between the black-box algorithmically personalized and reverse chronological feeds, however these works focus more on *what content* is being shown to users rather than *who* the users are being exposed to [4,12,13]. Social cues (e.g., the counts of likes and retweets a post has on Twitter/X) and the social context in which people share information (e.g., who they consider their audiences to be) have been shown to impact sharing behavior of posts on social media, and thus also impacts how information spreads [9,17]. To enable our understanding of how different recommender systems might shape users' perceptions of their network, we simulate a Twitter/X-like environment and measure the users' perceived prevalence of a binary trait in the network. With this we can consider how different kinds of feeds skew the perceived prevalence relative to the actual prevalence, which would indicate a bias in how users are exposed to their network.

In this paper we make the following contributions:

1. We present scalable agent-based model simulations with 173,000 nodes.
2. We compare perception biases generated from baselines, deep-learning approaches, and a novel greedy algorithm for personalizing news feeds.
3. We demonstrate that this greedy algorithm creates less biased feeds and makes feeds that are comparable in utility to the other tested models.

1 Related Work

This work can be categorized under social network simulations, recommender system analysis, and recommender system auditing, as we establish a framework that can be used to plug in and analyze how different implementations of recommender systems in personalized feeds work.

1.1 Social Network Simulations

Social network multi-agent simulations for recommender system analysis have been largely focused on information diffusion and predicting user behavior in different environmental circumstances. In Muric et al. [20] the authors utilize Twitter, Reddit and GitHub data to understand information spread, especially across different online platforms. This study did not explicitly focus on comparing different personalized feeds but rather focused on predicting information cascades in online environments.

Murdock et al. [19] simulated user and moderation behavior on Reddit to assess the impact of community-based networks and the unique moderation structure the platform has for belief diffusion.

Ribeiro, Veselovsky, and West [22] utilized an agent-based model to address the paradox that content-based recommender systems face: these systems do not seem to be the primary driver of what users consume even though they favor extreme content. When incorporating a measure of user utility in choosing which content to engage with, results suggest users will not engage with suggested low-utility content. Our work differs in that we compare different recommender systems and how they would behave considering the same user behavior patterns. Our work also considers platforms that use more social information in the recommendations, as a piece of content might appear in your feed if your friend interacts with it.

Donkers et al. [7] studied both epistemic and ideological echo chambers in social media and the effects of diversifying recommendations on discussions. They used knowledge graph embeddings to make diverse recommendations in a retweet network to depolarize discussions between users with varying propensities for accepting new information (i.e., retweeting something a peer posted). While depolarizing discussions is an important goal in this line of work, in our current study we simplify the models and compare their effect on perception instead.

1.2 Recommender System Audits

In general recommender system audits have been focused on content-based recommender systems as they are the most straightforward to analyze. In particular, most recent work has focused on YouTube and the role the video recommendation engine might have in spreading misinformation and radicalization. These works, like Tomlein et al. [24] and Hussein et al. [15] used agent-based sock puppets to simulate user behavior directly on the platform to measure the response in terms of personalization and prevalence of misinformation.

Both Spinelli and Crovella [23] and Ribeiro et al. [21] investigated YouTube's video recommender system and how it might contribute to gradual user radicalization. The latter study in particular analyzed user interactions and comments, focusing on migrations of users between communities. It is important to trace users in their experience on the platform to really understand how recommender systems and users interact. However, focusing on YouTube overlooks social signals: the same information may be perceived positively by a user if it was presented as being "liked" by a friend, but negatively by that user if it was presented by a stranger or someone they dislike. This makes such content-based studies about recommendations less relevant for platforms like X and Facebook.

1.3 Personalized News Feeds

Most studies investigating the effects of personalized news feeds, defined as the ordered information a user receives when logging onto a platform like X/Twitter, are focused around user satisfaction, impact on information diffusion, and echo chambers.

Two papers addressing perception and user satisfaction are Eslami et al. [10] and Eslami et al. [11], where tools were developed to study how users perceive the Facebook news feed algorithm at that time, i.e., they studied the impact of algorithmic awareness on user satisfaction and perception of their networks.

Bakshy et al. [3] from Facebook addressed information diffusion via the personalized News Feed by measuring user exposure to ideologically diverse posts. In this they considered how user preferences and algorithmic influence play a role in content consumption. They focused on the dynamics of information diffusion in Facebook's network at the time and did not emphasize the effect of different personalized news feeds.

More recently, Guess et al. [13] investigated the Facebook and Instagram feed algorithms and their potential impact on user attitude and election behavior in the 2020 presidential election. Gonzalez-Bailon et al. [12] studied the interaction of algorithmic curation and user social amplification by studying the spread of political URLs on Facebook, showing a segregated experience between liberal and conservative users. These papers are relevant to studying social network based recommendation systems, however they are focused on political content diffusion and political-behavior related outcomes for real users: our current study is concerned with comparing different types of personalized feeds and their impact on user exposure. This exposure is important as perception of the prevalence of traits in a network can potentially impact beliefs and behaviors related to those traits.

2 Model

2.1 Framework

We use the Repast framework to run models over a cluster of compute nodes [6]. This framework has previously been used in other areas like simulating bike-sharing systems in cities, and complex biological systems requiring heterogeneous multicellular organisms [2,18]. A key factor that aided our use of Repast is that in our simplified network, users will only be exposed to the tweets that their friends (and friends-of-friends) generate, which allows us to partition the network and run them in different processes.

2.2 User Behavior

In this work we trace the behavior of approximately 173,000 users (each who is labeled $x = 1$ with a fixed probability $P(X = 1)$ otherwise $x = 0$) sharing 1.5 million edges, and examine the experience of 5,599 central users as they follow the below sequence of events for each time tick t:

1. Activate user i with a uniform probability (0.083)
2. If activated, user i then produces a certain number of tweets; we sample a lognormal distribution ($\mu = 0.0, \sigma = 1.0$) to choose how many tweets the user produces in that time period
3. Add created tweets to the content pool
4. "Backend" model serves tweets to user i if appropriate
5. User i likes tweet from another user with same label at fixed probability (0.20), with probability (0.05) otherwise

Our model is a discrete event-based model, where for each time tick we "step" the individual nodes and then update model information before proceeding to the next time tick.

There are two key components for the model: the "backend" model that serves users tweets and the network of users. While each user is connected via the network, they only interact with other users on the network through the model by sending tweets to the model and getting tweets from their friends through the model. This way we can vary how tweets are served to users. We illustrate how this model works visually in Fig. 1.

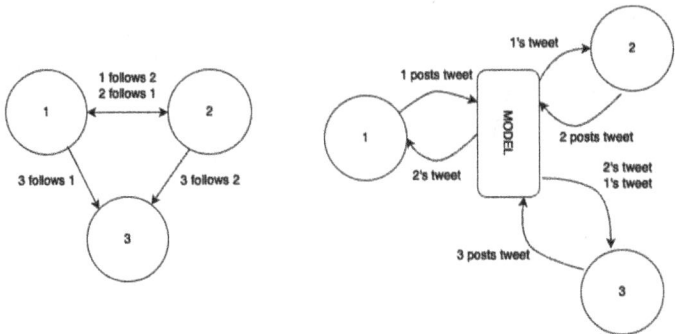

Fig. 1. Agent-based Model Structure Illustration demonstrating how three users are connected to each other on the network, but will only get exposed to other users through the tweets served to them from the "backend" model.

At tick $t = 24$ we reset the edges seen by users in the network to reflect a full 24 h passing, in order to assess what happens when the network "forgets" most information from the previous day.

We structure the network based on data from Alipourfard et al. [1] who gathered a complete follower network for 5,599 users, as well as tweets and retweets for those users and everyone they followed to generate a dataset with 4M users from May–September 2014. We use this data to guide our model; we downsample the nodes for the sake of simulation runtime.

2.3 Model Parameters

We treat each simulation time step as a single hour, for a total of 36 timesteps. Per an official blog-post from X [26], users spend an average of 32 min per day on the platform, which we implement in an activation probability: each user has a 0.083 probability of "logging in" per hour to give an expected value of approximately two sessions per 24 h.

To assess perception of networks, we randomly assign each user in the network a binary trait $X \in \{0, 1\}$ such that the total prevalence of the trait in the network is static. We run each simulation under $P(X = 1) \in \{0.05, 0.15, 0.50\}$ to assess the impact of the prevalence of the trait on the behavior of the system. Each user, based on the value of the trait that they are assigned, also behaves in a biased manner towards the tweets that they observe: users with $x = 1$ will like tweets from users with $x = 1$ with probability 0.20 and will like any other tweets with probability 0.05. Likewise for users with $x = 0$. Both numbers were chosen to elicit, in expectation, at least one like from each active user per tick.

Assigning traits to the nodes allows us to measure the degree-attribute correlation ρ_{kx}, which is defined as:

$$\rho_{kx} = \frac{P(x=1)}{\sigma_x \sigma_k}[\langle k \rangle_{x=1} - \langle k \rangle] \tag{1}$$

Here $\langle k \rangle_{x=1}$ is the average in-degree of the "active" $x = 1$ nodes, $\langle k \rangle$ is the average in-degree of all nodes considered, and σ represents the respective standard deviation.

Each simulation has every user subjected to the same personalized news feed:

1. **Random.** All candidate tweets are randomly sorted and the first n tweets are served to the user.
2. **Reverse Chronological.** All candidate tweets are sorted in reverse chronological order, and the first n tweets are served to the user.
3. **Neural Collaborative Filtering.** We implement a simple version of the Neural Collaborative Filtering (NCF) model to demonstrate how a deep learning model more broadly can be used for recommender systems in this context. We train the model on the 5,599 core users, where each tweet liked is the "item" being trained on. We keep the model straightforward and only use the superficial user level information [14].
4. **Wide & Deep.** We implement a simple version of the Wide & Deep model described initially by researchers at Google to demonstrate how a recommender system used in production in other contexts might behave in this scenario [5]. We use the same features as the NCF model for training.
5. **Minimize $\rho_{\mathbf{kx}}$.** We implement a greedy strategy for choosing which edges to observe for each user. We use Eq. 1 and sort the tweets seen by a user at every tick t by how much that edge would contribute to the difference between the mean "active" in-degree $\langle k \rangle_{x=1}$ and mean in-degree $\langle k \rangle$, opting for the edge that would minimize the difference.

We chose these personalized news feed algorithms to analyze different implementations of news feeds: there is a public release of the X recommendation "algorithm", however as it relies on multiple models and active services we cannot use the code as-is in a simulation (especially as production model parameters have since changed) [27]. Instead we aim to show simple baseline models, two deep-learning models, NCF and Wide & Deep, and our greedy strategy for minimizing exposure bias (MinimizeRho).

Each simulation similarly has every user using the same length feed, i.e., they only observe (and potentially engage) a fixed number of tweets for each timestep in the simulation. We tested lengths of 30, 50, and 100.

2.4 Bias and Performance Metrics

We use two metrics to study the bias of this perception:

1. Local Bias (B_{local}) $B_{\text{local}} = E[q_f(X)] - E[f(X)]$
2. Gini Coefficient (G) $G = \frac{\sum_{i=1}^{n}(2i-n-1)x_i}{n\sum_{i=1}^{n} x_i}$

We define B_{local} as the average frequency of the attribute among a node's immediate network: $E[q_f(X)] = \bar{d} * E[f(U)A(V)|(U,V) \sim \text{Uniform}(E)]$; $E[f(X)]$ is the global frequency of the node attribute f (here, 0.05, 0.15, 0.50); $f(U)$ the attribute value f of node U; $\bar{d}$ represents the expected in-degree of the network. $A(V)$ represents the "attention" node V pays to any node in their network. B_{local} should vary from $[-1,1]$, and Gini should vary from $[0,1]$, where 0 is equal and 1 is unequal. This plays the role of an overall view of the skew users will experience in their personalized feeds.

Gini coefficient in this context represents the skew in the number of unique friends (or friends-of-friends) users are exposed to in their feeds: x_i represents the number of times that friend (or friend-of-friend) was observed.

We use several other measurements to study the simulation and verify results (some not reported here):

1. **Precision@30.** mean $\left(\frac{|\text{tweets liked in first 30 positions}|}{30} \right)$
2. **Number of edges seen.** Total unique edges seen up until that time tick, including friends-of-friends.
3. **Mean number of likes friends' tweets receive.** We take the sum total likes each friend receives from core users and take the mean over all friends.

3 Results

Across models in Fig. 2 we observe relatively stable bias for the network until the reset at $t = 24$. Interestingly, we observe that the Random and MinimizeRho conditions have consistently low measures (in absolute value) of B_{local} (Local Bias). Similarly, the NCF and WideDeep conditions are correlated to one another, showing negative values (i.e., they under-expose the users to users with trait $X = 1$).

In Fig. 3 we observe converging, stable behavior of the Gini Coefficient, where the Random and Chronological conditions remain the lowest in terms of Gini, suggesting a more even distribution of attention across friends. Interestingly the MinimizeRho condition starts low and progresses higher to become similar to the Chronological, NCF, and WideDeep conditions. These two NCF and WideDeep models tend to have the highest Gini Coefficient, suggesting a narrower focus on sets of friends observed by users. This remains consistent even after the $t = 24$ reset where the MinimizeRho condition again starts low and progresses higher in Gini.

For validity checks of the simulations we present the results in Figs. 4 and 5. Figure 4 shows that the 5,599 core users all behave similarly under different conditions in terms of the number of tweets that they like cumulatively over the course of the simulation. The longer feed length simulations tend to have higher mean likes than the shorter ones. We observe similar behavior in the mean number of likes each friend receives, with longer feeds having higher mean tweets cumulatively over time. Finally we observe the unique edges observed by the core users in Fig. 5, where the Random condition maximize the total observed edges, followed by the MinimizeRho condition.

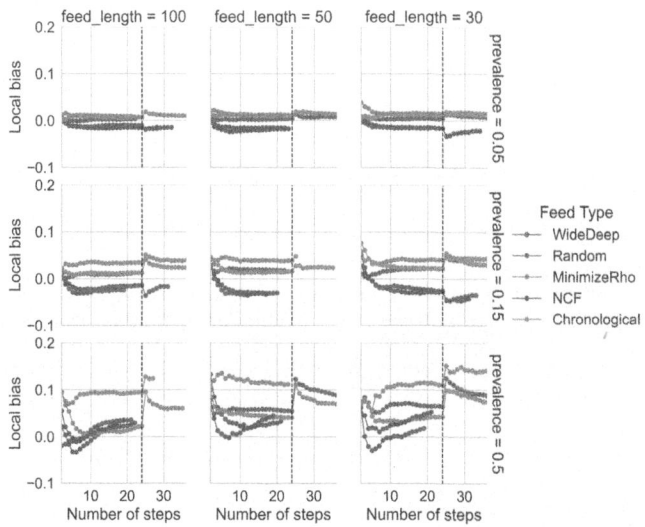

Fig. 2. Local Bias (B_{local}). Graph depicts the difference between the expected local fraction of friends who have $x = 1$ and the true global prevalence of the trait $P(X = 1)$. Positive implies over-representation, negative implies under-representation.

The precision figure in Fig. 6 demonstrates that all model conditions improve over time, with different levels of minor precision drop after the $t = 24$ reset.

4 Discussion

The information presented in Fig. 5 suggests that the Random and MinimizeRho conditions demonstrate the most growth in number of unique edges observed over time relative to the other models, increasing diversity in users who are observed. As this might be due to spurious changes in user behavior, we measure the mean number of likes each friend receives in Fig. 4. Here we observe that the longer feeds provides more likes for each friend, which follows given the increased number of "chances" each user would get to like a friend's tweet. Given each model has users that behave similarly, we then use the perception measures in Figs. 2 and 3 to determine differences between models. Two patterns show up: the Random and MinimizeRho conditions correlate closely and lower in absolute

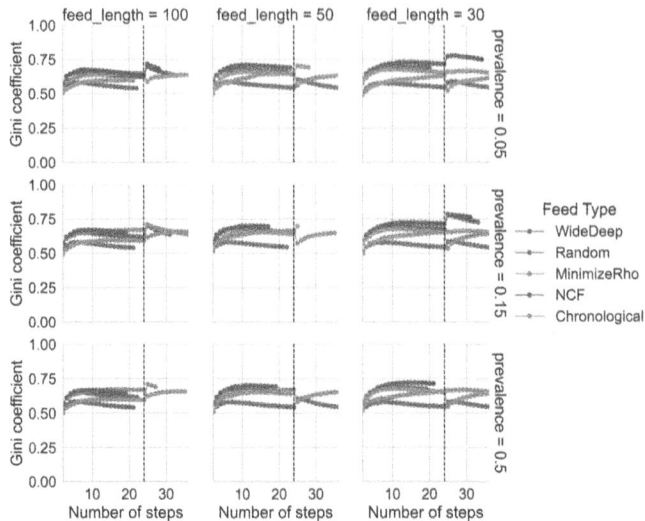

Fig. 3. Gini Coefficient. Graph depicts the distribution of times each friend (or friend-of-friend) was observed by a core user. 1 implies inequality, 0 implies equality.

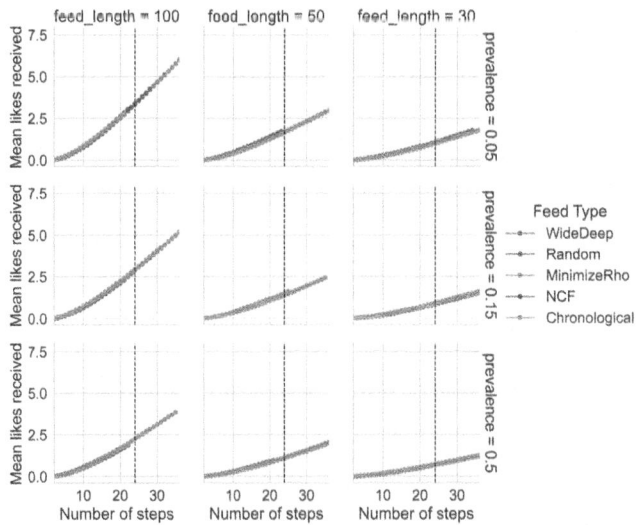

Fig. 4. Mean number of likes each friend receives. Graph depicts the mean number of likes each friend receives over time.

value in B_{local}, whereas the NCF and WideDeep models behave tightly, but with lower (negative) values in B_{local}. This suggests that the deep learning models are more tightly focused on certain sets of users (as corroborated in the number of edges seen in Fig. 5). Interestingly, the MinimizeRho condition behaves similarly to the Random condition in Fig. 3 in the initial timesteps, however it diverges

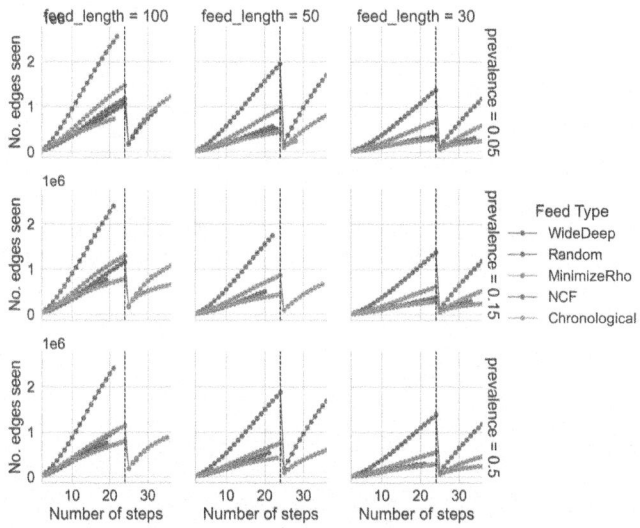

Fig. 5. Log number of friends seen. Graph depicts the log total number of unique friends (and friends-of-friends) seen through tick t. Connections seen are reset at $t = 24$.

and becomes more similar to the Chronological condition in most conditions (it becomes more like the deep learning models in the feed length of 100). This is interesting as it seems to be more sensitive to the feed length and prevalence than the other models tested in terms of Gini. This suggests that the MinimizeRho model converges to a similarly focused set of users as the deep learning models, but because it presents a comparatively undistorted view of the network the MinimzeRho model may be ignoring edges that might offer utility to users but skew the view of the network. If the Random model can be considered less biased than the others by minimizing the absolute value, then the MinimizeRho model seems to be most closely related to it in behavior over time (albeit in a more focused deterministic manner than the Random condition).

Curiously, each model trends upwards in performance in Precision@30 in Fig. 6. We would expect the Random model to have minimal slope as it does not depend on the user feedback, however, as the number of likes is stored cumulatively we would anticipate a growing number over time. The differences show themselves across different prevalences: $P(X = 1) = 0.05$ shows that the NCF model is seemingly higher than the other models in both measures of precision (Precision@10 not reported here), but the difference in models disappears as the prevalence of the trait tends towards $P(X = 1) = 0.50$. The drop in performance of the MinimizeRho model at feed length 50, $P(X = 1) = 0.15$ may be explained by the static assignments of the trait X for those simulations: other versions of these simulations where we modulate the correlation ρ_{kx} seems to remove this visible discrepancy.

Overall, while behavior of the simulated system appears to converge, it is unlikely that the real ecosystems being modeled would converge so readily. If

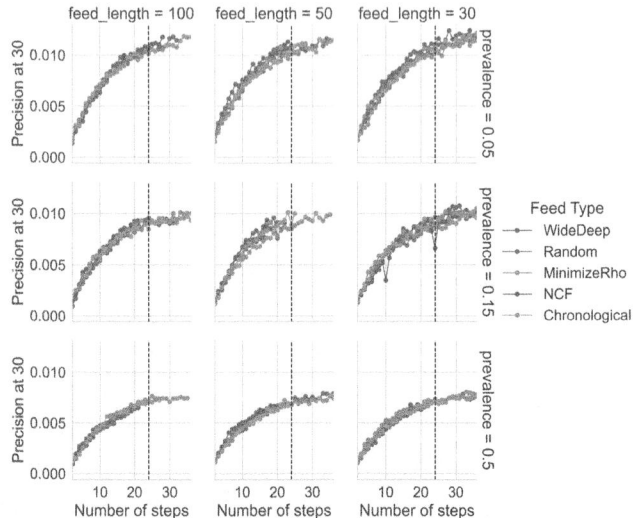

Fig. 6. Precision@30. Graph depicts the total fraction of liked tweets in the first 30 positions in the feed

we do assume some stability it seems to be the case that personalization would lead some users to perceive that any particular trait is more (or less) prevalent in their larger social networks than they actually are. In other words, it seems that personalization can either mitigate or amplify network-based structural phenomena like the majority illusion [16].

5 Limitations and Future Work

One clear limitation in our study is the duration for which we ran the simulations. Some of the more complex recommender feeds (and longer length feeds) took longer than expected to run. This is another limitation: we do not try more recommender systems and longer personalized feeds. There are advanced recommender systems that could be useful to analyze, like MV-DNN [8] or the stated X/Twitter system [27], however adapting such models is difficult as many require access to richer information about the users and content than we have built here (or for a production system we would need access to other microservices or models the system depends on). This complication aside, these more complex systems would afford us the ability to compare the results of these ABM studies more directly to real user studies, allowing us to tune the ABM parameters to be more accurate to real user behavior. However, it behooves us to be wary of running ABMs that are too contrived to be useful, as they can be difficult to reproduce and apply elsewhere.

Using Large Language Models as agents interacting in the framework would be interesting future work, considering Tornberg et al. [25] and their preliminary work in this space. This could facilitate the use of complicated recommender systems, as other ways of generating richer information would again potentially make the ABM too contrived to be useful, as described above.

We would also like to integrate more metrics into the analysis, as there may be confounding factors present in our simulations (e.g., B_{local} and G may converge but some other measure might be periodic). Similarly we would like to extend this analysis to more than binary user labels as labels can change over time and are often more complicated than simple binaries. In an effort for reproducibility we release the simulation scripts.[1]

6 Conclusion

In this work we describe an agent-based model and framework for studying the effects of different personalized news feed algorithms in online social networks by measuring how they expose users to their networks. The model and framework is extensible and given the underlying MPI usage of the underlying Repast library very scalable contingent upon having access to an MPI-enabled computing resource. We find that while deep learning methods are useful and tend to minimize perception bias in terms of our binary label, they focus on a narrower set of users. We find that a simple greedy algorithm based on network properties can relative diversity in attention and can minimize our measure of local perception bias B_{local} in absolute value.

These findings are important for designing recommender systems in online social networks that are robust: these systems mediate the information and connections between people and we should be able to understand what happens as people interact with these dynamic and ubiquitous systems.

Ethical Statement. We generally believe that agent-based models are an appropriate method for studying these systems in a way that preserves user privacy and dignity in this area of research. We do have concerns however that the more we understand recommender systems, the more of an attack vector we open up for malicious actors to manipulate these systems. Considering the recent (as of this writing) layoffs at major social media platforms, and a changing focus in Trust and Safety, this could pose a problem for the spread of harassment and misinformation.

References

1. Alipourfard, N., Nettasinghe, B., Abeliuk, A., Krishnamurthy, V., Lerman, K.: Friendship paradox biases perceptions in directed networks. Nat. Commun. **11**(1), 707 (2020)
2. Bae, J.W., Lee, C.H., Lee, J.W., Choi, S.H.: A data-driven agent-based simulation of the public bicycle-sharing system in Sejong City. Simul. Model. Pract. Theory **130**, 102861 (2024)

[1] https://github.com/bartleyn/cuddly-octo-couscous.

3. Bakshy, E., Messing, S., Adamic, L.A.: Exposure to ideologically diverse news and opinion on Facebook. Science **348**(6239), 1130–1132 (2015)
4. Bandy, J., Diakopoulos, N.: More accounts, fewer links: how algorithmic curation impacts media exposure in twitter timelines. Proc. ACM Hum.-Comput. Interact. **5**(CSCW1), 1–28 (2021)
5. Cheng, H.T., et al.: Wide & deep learning for recommender systems. In: Proceedings of the 1st Workshop on Deep Learning for Recommender Systems, pp. 7–10 (2016)
6. Collier, N., North, M.: Repast HPC: a platform for large-scale agent-based modeling. In: Large-Scale Computing, pp. 81–109 (2011)
7. Donkers, T., Ziegler, J.: The dual echo chamber: modeling social media polarization for interventional recommending. In: Proceedings of the 15th ACM Conference on Recommender Systems, pp. 12–22 (2021)
8. Elkahky, A.M., Song, Y., He, X.: A multi-view deep learning approach for cross domain user modeling in recommendation systems. In: Proceedings of the 24th International Conference on World Wide Web, pp. 278–288 (2015)
9. Epstein, Z., Lin, H., Pennycook, G., Rand, D.: How many others have shared this? Experimentally investigating the effects of social cues on engagement, misinformation, and unpredictability on social media. arXiv preprint arXiv:2207.07562 (2022)
10. Eslami, M., Aleyasen, A., Karahalios, K., Hamilton, K., Sandvig, C.: FeedVis: a path for exploring news feed curation algorithms. In: Proceedings of the 18th ACM Conference Companion on Computer Supported Cooperative Work & Social Computing, pp. 65–68 (2015)
11. Eslami, M., et al.: First i "like" it, then i hide it: folk theories of social feeds. In: Proceedings of the 2016 CHI Conference on Human Factors in Computing Systems, pp. 2371–2382 (2016)
12. González-Bailón, S., et al.: Asymmetric ideological segregation in exposure to political news on Facebook. Science **381**(6656), 392–398 (2023)
13. Guess, A.M., et al.: How do social media feed algorithms affect attitudes and behavior in an election campaign? Science **381**(6656), 398–404 (2023)
14. He, X., Liao, L., Zhang, H., Nie, L., Hu, X., Chua, T.S.: Neural collaborative filtering. In: Proceedings of the 26th International Conference on World Wide Web, pp. 173–182 (2017)
15. Hussein, E., Juneja, P., Mitra, T.: Measuring misinformation in video search platforms: an audit study on Youtube. Proc. ACM Hum.-Comput. Interact. **4**(CSCW1), 1–27 (2020)
16. Lerman, K., Yan, X., Wu, X.Z.: The "majority illusion" in social networks. PLoS ONE **11**(2), e0147617 (2016)
17. Marwick, A.E., Boyd, D.: I tweet honestly, i tweet passionately: Twitter users, context collapse, and the imagined audience. New Media Soc. **13**(1), 114–133 (2011)
18. Montagud, A., Ponce-de Leon, M., Valencia, A.: Systems biology at the giga-scale: large multiscale models of complex, heterogeneous multicellular systems. Curr. Opin. Syst. Biol. **28**, 100385 (2021)
19. Murdock, I., Carley, K.M., Yagan, O.: An agent-based model of reddit interactions and moderation (2023)
20. Murić, G., et al.: Large-scale agent-based simulations of online social networks. Auton. Agent. Multi-Agent Syst. **36**(2), 38 (2022)
21. Ribeiro, M.H., Ottoni, R., West, R., Almeida, V.A., Meira Jr, W.: Auditing radicalization pathways on Youtube. In: Proceedings of the 2020 Conference on Fairness, Accountability, and Transparency, pp. 131–141 (2020)

22. Ribeiro, M.H., Veselovsky, V., West, R.: The amplification paradox in recommender systems. In: Proceedings of the International AAAI Conference on Web and Social Media, vol. 17, pp. 1138–1142 (2023)
23. Spinelli, L., Crovella, M.: How Youtube leads privacy-seeking users away from reliable information. In: Adjunct Publication of the 28th ACM Conference on User Modeling, Adaptation and Personalization, pp. 244–251 (2020)
24. Tomlein, M., et al.: An audit of misinformation filter bubbles on Youtube: bubble bursting and recent behavior changes. In: Proceedings of the 15th ACM Conference on Recommender Systems, pp. 1–11 (2021)
25. Törnberg, P., Valeeva, D., Uitermark, J., Bail, C.: Simulating social media using large language models to evaluate alternative news feed algorithms. arXiv preprint arXiv:2310.05984 (2023)
26. X: One year in (2023). https://blog.twitter.com/en_us/topics/company/2023/one-year-in. Accessed 06 Apr 2024
27. X: Twitter github (2023). https://github.com/twitter/the-algorithm-ml. Accessed 06 Apr 2024

vivaFemme: Mitigating Gender Bias in Neural Team Recommendation via Female-Advocate Loss Regularization

Roonak Moasses[iD], Delaram Rajaei[iD], Hamed Loghmani[iD], Mahdis Saeedi[iD], and Hossein Fani[✉][iD]

University of Windsor, Windsor, ON, Canada
{moasses,rajaeid,ghasrlo,msaeedi,hfani}@uwindsor.ca

Abstract. Neural team recommendation has brought state-of-the-art efficacy while enhancing efficiency at forming teams of experts whose success in completing complex tasks is almost surely guaranteed. Yet proposed methods overlook diversity; that is, predicted teams are male-dominated and female participation is scarce. To this end, pre- and post-processing debiasing techniques have been initially proposed, mainly for being model-agnostic with little to no modification to the model's architecture. However, their limited mitigation performance has proven futile, especially in the presence of extreme bias, urging further development of *in*-process debiasing techniques. In this paper, we are the first to propose an in-process gender debiasing method in neural team recommendation via a novel modification to models' conventional cross-entropy loss function. Specifically, (1) we dramatically penalize the model (i.e., an increase to the loss) for false negative female experts, and meanwhile, (2) we randomly sample from female experts and reinforce the likelihood of female participation in the predicted teams, even at the cost of increasing false positive females. Our experiments on a benchmark dataset withholding extreme gender bias demonstrate our method's competence in mitigating gender bias in feed-forward neural models while maintaining accuracy. On the contrary, our method falls short of addressing bias in Bayesian models, urging further research on debiasing techniques for variational neural models. Our codebase to reproduce our experiments is available at https://github.com/fani-lab/OpeNTF/tree/vivaFemme-bias24.

Keywords: Fairness · Social Information Retrieval · OpeNTF

1 Introduction

As modern tasks have been surpassing the capacity of individuals, collaborative teams of experts have become vital in today's diverse landscape across academia, industry, law, freelancing, and healthcare. The team recommendation problem, also known as team allocation, team selection, team composition, and team configuration, seeks to automate the assembly of experts in a team whose combined skills solve challenging tasks. Team recommendation can be seen as social

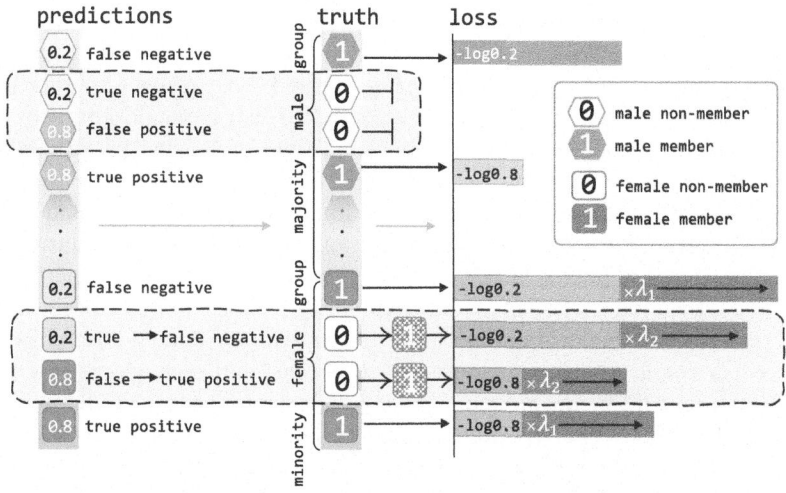

Fig. 1. Female-advocate loss regularization. (Color figure online)

information retrieval (Social IR), where the right group of experts, rather than relevant information, is required to accomplish the task at hand.

Traditionally, even now in many scientific and industrial sectors, teams have been formed manually by relying on human experience and instinct, a process that is tedious, error-prone, and suboptimal due to hidden personal and societal biases, a multitude of criteria to optimize, and an overwhelming number of candidates, among other reasons. Notably, the team formation has been heavily influenced by the individuals' subjective opinions which inherit hidden and unfair societal biases, largely ignoring the diversity in recommending expert members of a team, resulting in discrimination and reduced visibility for already disadvantaged *female* experts [11], disproportionate selection of *male* experts, and gender disparities [14].

Within the vast space of expert combinations, machine learning, neural models in particular, have enabled the analysis of massive collections of experts from diverse fields through learning relationships between experts and their skills based on past teams' successes and failures [6,7,19]. However, machine learning-based methods of team recommendation focus solely on maximizing the teams' success rates, overlooking fairness and diversity among team members. Such recommended teams are often successful yet unfair and biased toward the predominant distribution of male experts in the training datasets, with females heavily underrepresented. For example, in the imdb dataset for movies, 87.7% of the cast and crew are male compared to 12.3% female. Therefore, male cast and crew receive more attention and are more frequently recommended by a machine learning model, leading to discrimination against already disadvantaged female experts. To the best of our knowledge, there is no fairness-aware approach in the neural team recommendation method except that of Loghmani et al. [16], who showed *post*-processing greedy rerankers falls short of maintaining the accuracy of recommended teams when mitigating the popularity bias, urging further tandem integration of *in*-process debiasing techniques. In this paper, we propose viva*F*emme, an *in*-process debiasing method with respect to the demographic (statistical) parity [17] where the model's recommendation of experts are *in*dependent of their genders. As opposed to pre-processing-based methods, which modify data or its labels before model training via over/under sampling, or post-processing techniques, which seek to improve the fairness of models after training via reranking experts in the final ranked list of recommendations, we focus on balancing model accuracy with fairness considerations during training by adjusting the model's loss in favour of minority female experts. Specifically, in *neural* team recommendation models, where the team recommendation has been addressed as a *multilabel* Boolean classification task, and each expert is mapped to a label and would be recommended should the expert's class prediction probability be close to one, (1) we dramatically penalize the model by a substantial increase to the loss if a false negative happens for a female expert, i.e., a female expert who is a member of an optimum team has been overlooked by the model, compared to when the false negative happens for a male expert. For example, from Fig. 1, a true female member (red square 1), which has not been recommended for low probability 0.2, generates an increased loss of $-\lambda_1 \times \log 0.2$ compared to its male peer (blue hexagon 1). Additionally, given a *fixed* number of false positive experts by a model, i.e., incorrect recommendation of experts who are *not* members of an optimum team, skewing false positives toward *female* experts neither helps nor hurts the accuracy more, yet improves the participation of minority female experts in the recommended teams. In view of this presumption, (2) we randomly sample from female experts who are not part of an optimum team as if they should have been in the team and reinforce the likelihood of their participation in the recommended teams by adding their loss values to the original training loss at the cost of increasing false positives but in favour of female experts. For example, from Fig. 1, there are two female and two male experts who are not members of an optimum team (white squares 0 and white hexagons 0, respectively). While these male experts have contributed no loss even if the model recommended one of them for the high probability 0.8 (false positive), the female experts have been *virtually* considered members of the optimum team and contributed increased loss values by the factor of λ_2. To illustrate the effectiveness of our proposed female-advocate loss, we perform experiments on a benchmark dataset (imdb). Our results show that our proposed loss substantially mitigates gender bias while maintaining the accuracy of the recommended teams in feed-forward neural architectures. However, it falls short of mitigating bias when plugged into variational Bayesian neural models, urging further research on in-process loss-based bias mitigation techniques for such architectures.

2 Related Works

The works related to this paper are largely centered around two areas: 1) neural team recommendation and 2) fairness-aware recommendation.

2.1 Neural Team Recommendation

Thus far, proposed machine learning-based solutions to the team recommendation problem are based on neural models that can be categorized based on their model architecture, including feed-forward, variational Bayesian networks [6], and graph neural networks, and training strategies including negative sampling [6] heuristics and streaming (temporal) training [8]. Sapienza et al. [20] were the first to use graph representations learning in the form of an autoencoder for the team recommendation problem in online multiplayer games. They propose to learn dense vector representations for game players (experts) via random walks on the co-play network upon which pairwise top-k closest vector representation of experts yields the optimum subset of experts as a team. Sapienza et al.'s method, however, builds autoencoder models independently for each game, resulting in player-specific vector representations for each game and overlooking the joint combination of proficiencies. Other researchers have explored alternative neural architectures. Rad et al. [19] proposed variational Bayesian neural model incorporating uncertainty via probabilistic weights to address overfitting. They employ a multi-layer feed-forward neural network to map the required subset of skills to an optimum subset of experts as the recommended team. Later, Rad et al. [18] used a graph neural network to learn dense vector representation of skills at the input layer of variational Bayesian neural model and showed performance improvements. In the neural team recommendation literature, (non-variational) feed-forward neural networks have also been employed as a baseline to provide a reference level of comparison [6]. Reinforcement learning via neural policy estimators has also been proposed to emulate team formation processes in multi-agent environments, where autonomous agents learn to negotiate and decide team composition for tasks that individual agents cannot complete alone [3].

Despite the rich body of research, existing neural team recommendation models overlook fairness. Meanwhile, accounting for fairness has gained significant importance in other disciplines such as healthcare [5], information retrieval [4], computer vision, ranking and recommendations. In this paper, we are among the first to undertake an empirical investigation addressing the fairness gap in neural team recommendation by assessing the impact of loss regularization in favor of recommending more female experts while controlling the accuracy of the recommended teams.

2.2 Fairness-Aware Recommendation

Fairness in machine learning has been addressed at an individual level, where consistency in treatment toward an individual is expected, and at a group level, where equitable treatment is sought between a disadvantaged (protected) group and the advantaged group as a whole, e.g., female vs. male experts. Fairness-aware approaches aim to identify and assess unfair biases or mitigate them through debiasing algorithms at individual or group levels.

Debiasing algorithms can be categorized based on their integration into the machine learning pipeline: (1) pre-processing methods modify data or labels through re-sampling heuristics before model training, (2) in-processing techniques adjust the optimization process of models to balance accuracy and fairness, and (3) post-processing methods modify model outputs during inference, which may involve altering thresholds, scoring rules, or reranking the recommended list of items. Since preprocessing methods entail significant alterations to datasets, particularly when confronted with extreme biases, and re-sampling adjustments may result in deviation from real-world scenarios, researchers mostly opt for in-processing and post-processing methods. For instance, Zehlike et al. [21] proposed an in-process method by extending the loss function of ListNet, a list-wise learning-to-rank model, with fairness objective based on reducing the discrepancy in average group visibility (exposure) between a protected group and a non-protected group in the ranking results. From post-processing methods, Feng et al. [9] studied gender bias associated with professional occupations in search results across major search engines and developed a re-ranking algorithm that prioritizes gender parity in top positions while maintaining relevance.

While there are few studies in fairness-aware team recommendation literature such as the work by Barnabò et al. [2] that proposed *search*-based greedy approximation for a fair team through the weighted set cover problem, there is no fairness-aware method that mitigates unfair gender bias in machine learning-based team recommendation except that of the work by Loghmani et al. [16] that showed existing greedy post-processing reranking methods fall short of mitigating neural team recommendation models' bias toward popularity experts "while maintaining models' accuracy". To bridge this research gap, we present a unique contribution yet pioneering in-process method for machine learning-based team recommendation.

3 Female-Advocate Neural Team Recommendation

In this section, we foremost provide a formal problem statement for neural team recommendation, on the one hand, and demographic parity notions of fairness, on the other hand. Then, we formalize our proposed in-process loss-based method for neural team recommendation to recommend an optimum yet fair team of experts with respect to gender bias in view of demographic parity.

3.1 Neural Team Recommendation

Given a set of skills $\mathcal{S} = \{i\}$ and a set of experts $\mathcal{E} = \{j\}$, an optimum team of experts $\mathbf{e} \subseteq \mathcal{E}$; $\mathbf{e} \neq \emptyset$ that collectively cover the skill set $\mathbf{s} \subseteq \mathcal{S}$; $\mathbf{s} \neq \emptyset$ is shown by $(\mathbf{s}, \mathbf{e})$. Further, $\mathcal{T} = \{(\mathbf{s}, \mathbf{e}) | \mathbf{s} \subseteq \mathcal{S}, \mathbf{e} \subseteq \mathcal{E}\}$ indexes all optimum teams. For a given subset of desired skills $\mathbf{s}$, the goal of the team recommendation problem is to recommend an optimal subset of experts $\mathbf{e}$ that their collaboration as a team leads to success, i.e., $(\mathbf{s}, \mathbf{e}) \in \mathcal{T}$, while avoiding a potentially unsuccessful subset of experts $\mathbf{e}'$, i.e., $(\mathbf{s}, \mathbf{e}') \notin \mathcal{T}$. More concretely, the team recommendation problem is to find a mapping function $\mathcal{F}$ of parameters θ from the power set of skills to the power set of experts such that $\mathcal{F}_\theta : \mathcal{P}(\mathcal{S}) \rightarrow \mathcal{P}(\mathcal{E}), \mathcal{F}_\theta(\mathbf{s}) = \mathbf{e}$.

Neural team recommendation estimates $\mathcal{F}_\theta(\mathbf{s})$ using a multilayer neural network that learns, from $\mathcal{T}$, to map a vector representation of subset of skills $v_\mathbf{s}$, to a vector representation of subset of experts v_e by maximizing the posterior probability of $\boldsymbol{\theta}$ in $\mathcal{F}_{\boldsymbol{\theta}}$ over $\mathcal{T}$, that is, $\mathrm{argmax}_{\boldsymbol{\theta}}\, p(\boldsymbol{\theta}|\mathcal{T})$. For v_s, neural team recommendation methods adopt either (1) the *occurrence* vector representation for **s** or (2) a dense low d-dimensional vector representation of **s**, $d << |\mathcal{S}|$, pretrained by e.g., a graph neural network [12]. In the output layer for vector representation of the subset of experts v_e, neural team recommendation methods frame the problem as a *multilabel* Boolean classification task and used occurrence vector representation for **e**, that is, $v_e \in \{0,1\}^{|\mathcal{E}|}$ where $v_e[j] = 1$ if $j \in \mathbf{e}$, and 0 otherwise, as seen in Fig. 1. Using a neural model of one hidden layer **h** of size d, without loss of generality to multiple hidden layers, with the input layer v_s and output layer v_e, a neural team recommendation method can be formalized as,

$$\mathbf{h} = \pi(\boldsymbol{\theta}_1 v_s + \mathbf{b}_1) \quad (1)$$
$$logits \to \mathbf{z} = \boldsymbol{\theta}_2 \mathbf{h} + \mathbf{b}_2 \quad (2)$$
$$v_e = \sigma(\mathbf{z}) \quad (3)$$

where π is a nonlinear activation function, $\boldsymbol{\theta} = \boldsymbol{\theta}_1 \cup \boldsymbol{\theta}_2 \cup \mathbf{b}_1 \cup \mathbf{b}_2$ are learnable parameters for $\mathcal{F}$, and σ is the sigmoid function to interpret the model's output as each expert's predicted probability of membership in **e**. During training, given a team $(\mathbf{s}, \mathbf{e})$, neural models tune the parameters $\boldsymbol{\theta}$ by maximizing the posterior probability of $\boldsymbol{\theta}$ in $\mathcal{F}_{\boldsymbol{\theta}}$ over $\mathcal{T}$. By Bayes theorem:

$$\mathrm{argmax}_{\boldsymbol{\theta}}\, p(\boldsymbol{\theta}|\mathcal{T}) \propto p(\mathcal{T}|\boldsymbol{\theta})p(\boldsymbol{\theta}) = p(\boldsymbol{\theta}) \prod_{(\mathbf{s},\mathbf{e}) \in \mathcal{T}} p(\mathbf{e}|\mathbf{s}, \boldsymbol{\theta}) \quad (4)$$

where $p(\mathcal{T})$ is independent of $\boldsymbol{\theta}$, $p(\mathcal{T}|\boldsymbol{\theta})$ is the likelihood and can be estimated via average *binary* cross-entropy over $\mathbf{e}$:

$$p(\mathbf{e}|\mathbf{s}, \boldsymbol{\theta}) = \prod_{j \in \mathbf{e}} \sigma(\mathbf{z}[j]) \propto \sum_{j \in \mathbf{e}} \log \sigma(\mathbf{z}[j]) \quad (5)$$

and $p(\boldsymbol{\theta})$ is the prior joint probability of weights, which is unknown. The *true* prior probability of weights $p(\boldsymbol{\theta})$ cannot be calculated analytically or efficiently sampled, and as such, existing works either assume the *uniform* probability distribution over all possible real-values of $\boldsymbol{\theta}$ and proceed with maximum likelihood estimation $p(\mathcal{T}|\boldsymbol{\theta})$ [6] using (non-variational) feed-forward neural model, or estimate $p(\boldsymbol{\theta})$ by Gaussian distribution and calculate the maximum a posterior via a variational Bayesian neural model [12,13].

Nonetheless, existing loss-based optimizations are prone to overfitting male experts when training data suffers from a dominant distribution of male experts in successful teams, and the female experts have participated sparingly, reinforcing the unfair gender disparity.

3.2 Demographic Parity

To eschew varied interpretations and to provide actionable criteria to design and evaluate fairness-aware methods, fairness has been mathematically formalized,

Table 1. Statistics of the imdb.

	raw	filtered
#teams	507,034	32,059
#unique experts	876,981	2,011
#unique female experts	-	248
#unique male experts	-	1,763
#unique skills	28	23
#team w/ single expert	322,918	0
#team w/ single skill	315,503	15,180
avg #expert per team	1.88	3.98
avg #female expert per team	-	0.01
avg #male expert per team	-	3.91
avg #skill per team	1.54	1.76
avg #team per expert	1.09	62.45
avg #skill per expert	1.59	10.85

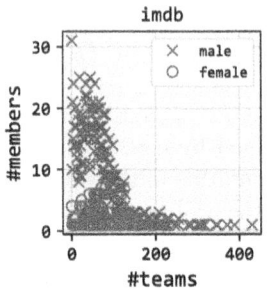

Fig. 2. Sparse vs. dominant distribution of female and male experts.

with a level of abstraction from an underlying real-world scenario, based on well-known notions of justice and equity at a group level, like females vs. males, including demographic parity, equality of odds, and equality of opportunity. In this paper, we focus on the *demographic parity* notion of fairness and defer the exploration of other notions to future work.

Given the protected attribute *gender* of values $\{f : \text{female}, m : \text{male}\}$, we divide experts into the protected groups of $\mathcal{G}_f = \{j_f\} \subseteq \mathcal{E}$ and $\mathcal{G}_m = \{j_m\} \subseteq \mathcal{E}$ for female experts vs. male ones. Given D the set of decisions, demographic parity requires a decision $d \in D$ for members of protected groups to be *in*dependent of the value of the protected attribute [17]. Formally,

$$\forall d \in D : p(\hat{d}|j_f) = p(\hat{d}|j_m) \tag{6}$$

where $\hat{d}$ is the predicted decision for the correct decision d. In fair team recommendation, decisions are about the Boolean membership status of experts in the recommended subset of experts $\mathbf{e}$, i.e., $j \in \mathbf{e}$ or $j \notin \mathbf{e}$. Hence, Eq. 6 becomes:

$$\forall j_f \in \mathcal{G}_f, j_m \in \mathcal{G}_m; \overbrace{[p(j_f \in \mathbf{e}) = p(j_m \in \mathbf{e})]}^{\text{true positives}} \wedge \overbrace{[p(j_f \notin \mathbf{e}) = p(j_m \notin \mathbf{e})]}^{\text{true negatives}} \tag{7}$$

Intuitively, demographic parity enforces the membership in a team to be independent of values of the protected attribute for team members, i.e., no regard to their gender or any other protected characteristics.

From Eq. 5, neural team recommendation methods calculate the loss values only for those who should be members of the optimum team, i.e., $j \in \mathbf{e}$ or true positives, primarily for training efficiency, overlooking $j \notin \mathbf{e}$ or true negatives in Eq. 7; The number of experts in an optimum team $|\mathbf{e}|$, is significantly less than the number of unique experts $|\mathcal{E}|$, i.e., $|\mathbf{e}| \ll |\mathcal{E}|$ as in imdb where $3.98 \ll 2,011$, hence, calculating the loss for experts who should *not* be in the optimum team, i.e., $j \notin \mathbf{e}$ or true negatives, for every training samples would be computationally prohibitive. Secondly, even for the true positives in Eq. 7, their loss function

(Eq. 5) is oblivious to the prior distribution of female and male experts in the training datasets. Therefore, the dominant distribution of male experts in training instances of teams results in higher loss values and further frequent updates to the neural model's parameters but for male experts, leaving little to no update for female experts due to their sparse distribution in teams.

3.3 viva.Femme: Female-Advocate Loss Regularization

The overarching theme of our paper is to propose a gender-aware loss function that advocates the minority protected group, herein, the female experts $\mathcal{G}_f$, to dampen the effect of the majority protected group, i.e., the male experts $\mathcal{G}_m$. We propose viva.Femme, which modifies the original loss in Eq. 5 via two regularization components with respect to Eq. 7, as explained hereafter.

Foremost, we make a distinction for the loss values of female and male expert members of an optimum team, i.e., $\mathbf{e} = \{j_f \in \mathbf{e}\} \cup \{j_m \in \mathbf{e}\}$, or female true positives vs. male ones. For female experts $j_f \in \mathbf{e}$, given their very sparse distribution in teams in a biased dataset, thereby very low probability of their encounter during a model training, we drastically penalize the model by amplifying the loss values via a punitive coefficient λ_1 should it miss the correct recommendations for such scarce and invaluable opportunities. In contrast, the model expects frequent encounters with male experts during training, whose accumulative loss values over many teams would provide sufficient guides toward their correct recommendations. In doing so, we strictly avoid the model's tendency to under-represent female experts in the optimum teams and provide a balance in the true positive part of Eq. 7. Formally,

$$p(\mathbf{e}|\mathbf{s},\boldsymbol{\theta}) \propto \underbrace{\sum_{j_m \in \mathbf{e}} \log \sigma(\mathbf{z}[j_m])}_{\text{male true positives}} + \underbrace{\sum_{j_f \in \mathbf{e}} \lambda_1 \times \log \sigma(\mathbf{z}[j_f])}_{\text{female true positives}} \qquad (8)$$

Next, with regard to the true negatives in Eq. 7, we assume that given a *fixed* number of false recommendations of experts, a model that incorrectly recommends more female experts than male experts is preferable, because, while it yields the same performance drain, it advocates more participation of female experts in teams. Indeed, in a biased dataset with a predominant distribution of male experts, not only does the model become biased toward recommending more male experts under the binary cross-entropy, but also produces more false recommendations of male experts and, hence, unbalancing the true negatives part of the Eq. 7. To counter, we enforce a neural model to recommend more female experts for an optimum team, even incorrectly and knowing the cost of female false positives (which is negligible in view of a male-dominant dataset), by considering random samples of female experts who are *not* members of the optimum team as *virtually* correct members of the team, i.e., $j'_f \notin \mathbf{e} \rightarrow j'_f \in^* \mathbf{e}$ and calculate their losses by a punitive coefficient λ_2. Hence, should a neural model falsely recommend incorrect experts, it favours female experts over male experts. Formally,

$$p(\mathbf{e}|\mathbf{s},\boldsymbol{\theta}) \propto \sum_{j_m \in \mathbf{e}} \log \sigma(\mathbf{z}[j_m]) + \sum_{j_f \in \mathbf{e}} \lambda_1 \times \log \sigma(\mathbf{z}[j_f]) + \overbrace{\sum_{j'_f \sim \mathbb{P}: j'_f \notin \mathbf{e}} \lambda_2 \times \log \sigma(\mathbf{z}[j'_f])}^{\text{female false negatives}} \quad (9)$$

where $\mathbb{P}$ is the probability distribution from which we draw k female experts j_f as *virtually* correct member of the optimum team $(\mathbf{s}, \mathbf{e})$ where $j_f \in \mathbf{e}$ but $j'_f \notin \mathbf{e}$.

4 Experiments

We present our experiments to answer the following research questions:
RQ1: Can our proposed loss function mitigate the gender bias in neural team recommendation methods while maintaining models' accuracy?
RQ2: Is the proposed loss's impact consistent across different desired distributions of female vs. male experts in the recommended teams?
RQ3: To what extent does the random sampling of female experts contribute to gender bias mitigation?

4.1 Setup

Dataset. We assess viva*F*emme's effectiveness on imdb, a widely recognized benchmark dataset within the domain of team recommendation [6], where each entry is a moving picture such as a movie or a tv series including the top-10 short-listed cast and crew such as directors, producers, actors and actresses. We consider each movie as an optimum team, which has been successfully produced, the cast and crew as the team members, and the genres as the skills of the team. It's important to note that the utilization of imdb in team recommendation literature differs from its applications in movie recommender systems or movie review analysis; our objective here is to assemble teams of cast and crew for movie *production* rather than movie recommendation. For the cast and crew's gender labels, we inferred the gender of some cast and crew by their role identified as actor or actress. For the rest, we utilized genderize [1]. We filtered out singleton and sparse teams with less than 3 members, as suggested by [19]. Table 1 reports statistics on the raw and filtered dataset. Also, as seen in Fig. 2, male experts are dominating teams while female experts have participated sparingly.

Baselines. We compare the impact of our proposed loss function on mitigating the gender bias of two reference neural architectures: (1) feed-forward non-Bayesian (non-variational) neural network (fnn) [6,19] and (2) the-state-of-the-art Bayesian (variational) neural network (bnn). Both models include a single hidden layer of size d=128 and leaky relu is the activation function for the hidden layer. For the input layer, we used sparse occurrence vector representations (multi-hot encoded) of skills of size $|\mathcal{S}|$. The output layer is the sparse occurrence vector representations (multi-hot encoded) of experts of size $|\mathcal{E}|$. We trained the neural models using the binary cross-entropy (xe) as the biased baseline, viva♀emme without random samplings of female experts (vf_), and viva♀emme with random sampling (vf) of $k = |\mathcal{G}_f|$ female experts from $\mathbb{P}$ =uniform distribution for increasing punitive coefficients $\lambda_1 = \lambda_2 = \lambda \in \{2, 4, 8 \ldots, 128\}$.

4.2 Evaluation Strategy and Metrics

We randomly select 15% of teams for the test set and perform 5-fold cross-validation on the remaining teams for model training and validation that results in one trained model per fold. Given an optimum team $(\mathbf{s}, \mathbf{e})$ from the test set, we compare the top-k ranked list of experts, recommended by the model of each fold, with the observed subset of experts $\mathbf{e}$ and report the average accuracy of models on all folds in terms of normalized discounted cumulative gain (ndcg), mean average precision (map), and precision (p) at top-10 as well as area under the receiver operating characteristic (aucroc). In all such metrics, the higher value indicates more accurate recommendations.

To evaluate fairness, we used ndkl [10], which measures the *divergence* of the distribution of a protected group in the ranked list of recommendations with the ideal fair distribution using Kullback-Leibler [15], and the lower divergence the better with being 0 in the ideal equal distributions. We measure ndkl for increasing ratios of 0.1 to 0.9 for female experts as the ideal fair distributions.

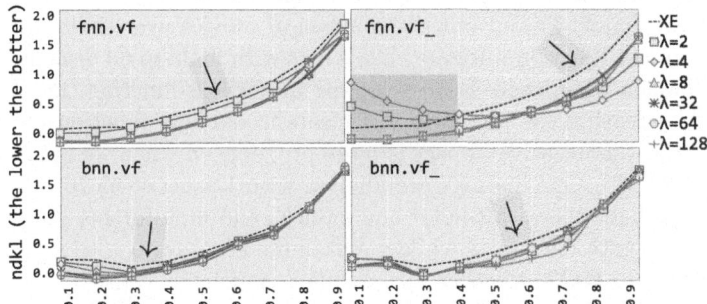

Fig. 3. Comparative fairness results for an increasing ratio of female experts.

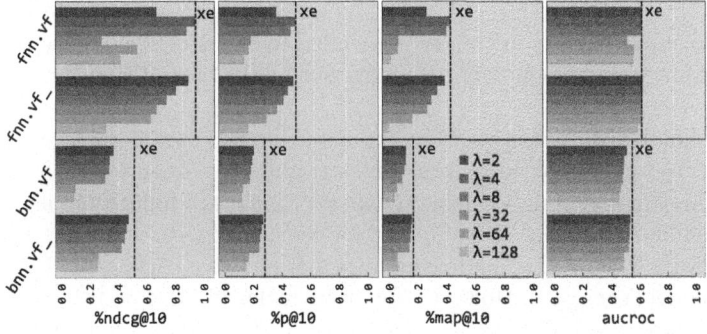

Fig. 4. Comparative accuracy results with sampling and lack thereof.

4.3 Result

In response to **RQ1**, from Fig. 3 (left), we observe that our proposed loss with random sampling consistently yields less divergence across increasing desired ratios of female experts in the recommended teams, hence, better fairness compared to the binary cross-entropy (xe) across neural models and increasing punitive coefficients. For instance, at the ideal ratio of 0.9 where we expect to observe 90% female experts, not unexpectedly, all loss functions fall short of reaching the ideal distribution, yet our loss function obtains closer distribution across increasing values of λ. For lower ratios, like 0.5 where we expect a balance between female and male experts in the recommended teams, while all loss functions have been more or less effective, viva.Femme is the most effective one across different punitive coefficients in both bnn and fnn models. Further, from Fig. 4 and for fnn, we can observe that viva.Femme with sampling (fnn.vf) could obtain the fairest distributions for different ideal ratios of female experts yet maintaining success rate in terms of accuracy metrics for $\lambda = 4$ or with a minor decrease for $\lambda = 8$. Based on our observations from Fig. 3 (left) and Fig. 4, we can conclude that viva.Femme can mitigate the unfair gender bias against female experts in feed-forward neural team recommendation methods while maintaining the model's accuracy. Looking at the Bayesian neural model in Fig. 4 (bnn.*), we foremost observe its generally poor performance compared to fnn, as already shown by Dashti et al. [6], which has been attributed to the small number of skills (genres of movies) and fair distribution of movies over skills. In contrast with fnn, our loss function mitigates bnn's bias with little to no discounts on the model's accuracy when there is *no* sampling in our loss function (bnn.vf_). As seen, while increasing the punitive coefficients in our loss function reduces the bnn's accuracy, the negative impact is more pronounced when we apply random sampling (bnn.vf). Our findings are aligned with Dashti et al. [6] where sampling methods have shown futile for bnn models, and urge further study for loss function to mitigate bnn's bias while maintaining accuracy.

In response to **RQ2**, whether viva.Femme's impact is consistent across different desired distributions of female experts in the recommended teams, from Fig. 3, we observe a consistent trend of lower ndkl values for our method across neural models and increasing ratios from 0.1 to 0.9, compared to the binary cross-entropy (xe). Therefore, viva.Femme is effective for different desired distributions of female experts in the recommended teams. However, as we mentioned in **RQ1**, bnn.* recommends fairer teams but at the cost of slightly lower accuracy.

Regarding **RQ3**, that is, to what extent each of the viva.Femme's component contribute to its effectiveness, from Fig. 3 (right), we observe that viva.Femme without random sampling for female experts (fnn.vf_) follows similar trend as in viva.Femme with random sampling for female experts (fnn.vf) from ideal ratios above 0.4 across the increasing range of punitive coefficients (λ) for feed-forward model (fnn.vf_). However, for lower ratios like 0.1 to 0.3, viva.Femme without random sampling for female experts (fnn.vf_) yields higher values of ndkl and falls short of providing the desired distribution in fnn. Moreover, from

Fig. 4, fnn.vf_ fails to maintain the model's performance across accuracy metrics and increasing values of punitive coefficients, except that of $\lambda = 2$. Therefore, while the effort by the viva𝓕emme without positive sampling is noteworthy, it is insufficient, and the random sampling component is critically required for viva𝓕emme's consistent mitigation of unfair gender bias.

For the Bayesian model (bnn.*), our loss function, with and without random sampling, has lower ndkl, hence, better fairness across all coefficients. However, its positive impact on fairness is marginal compared to the binary cross-entropy baseline (xe), indicating further research on loss functions for variational models.

5 Conclusion

In this paper, we addressed gender bias in neural team recommendation models via an in-process loss-based method. Wherein we substantially penalize the model for failing to recommend true female expert members while promoting more female inclusion by favoring them over male experts in case of incorrect recommendations. Our experiments on the imdb dataset demonstrate the effectiveness of our approach in debiasing gender disparities in feed-forward neural models while maintaining accuracy. For variational Bayesian neural models, while our proposed loss function reduces gender bias, it comes at a slight accuracy reduction. Future work involves developing an in-process method to mitigate gender bias in variational models as well as studying our method under other notions of fairness, e.g., equality of opportunity, on datasets from diverse domains like patents and (uspt) and open-source software (github).

References

1. https://genderize.io/. Accessed 16 June 2023
2. Barnabò, G., Fazzone, A., Leonardi, S., Schwiegelshohn, C.: Algorithms for fair team formation in online labour marketplaces10033. In: WWW (2019)
3. Bachrach, Y.: Negotiating team formation using deep reinforcement learning. Artif. Intell. **288**, 103356 (2020). https://doi.org/10.1016/J.ARTINT.2020.103356
4. Bigdeli, A., Arabzadeh, N., SeyedSalehi, S., Zihayat, M., Bagheri, E.: Gender fairness in information retrieval systems. In: SIGIR 2022 (2022)
5. Chen, R.J., et al.: Algorithmic fairness in artificial intelligence for medicine and healthcare. Nat. Biomed. Eng. (2023)
6. Dashti, A., Samet, S., Fani, H.: Effective neural team formation via negative samples. In: CIKM (2022)
7. Dashti, A., Saxena, K., Patel, D., Fani, H.: OpeNTF: a benchmark library for neural team formation. In: CIKM (2022)
8. Fani, H., Barzegar, R., Dashti, A., Saeedi, M.: A training strategy for future collaborative team prediction. In: ECIR (2024)
9. Feng, Y., Shah, C.: Has CEO gender bias really been fixed? Adversarial attacking and improving gender fairness in image search. In: Proceedings of the AAAI Conference on Artificial Intelligence (2022)

10. Geyik, S.C., Ambler, S., Kenthapadi, K.: Fairness-aware ranking in search & recommendation systems with application to LinkedIn talent search. In: KDD, pp. 2221–2231. ACM (2019)
11. Hajian, S., Bonchi, F., Castillo, C.: Algorithmic bias: from discrimination discovery to fairness-aware data mining. In: SIGKDD, pp. 2125–2126 (2016)
12. Hamidi Rad, R., Bagheri, E., Kargar, M., Srivastava, D., Szlichta, J.: Retrieving skill-based teams from collaboration networks. In: SIGIR 2021. Association for Computing Machinery (2021)
13. Hamidi Rad, R., Fani, H., Bagheri, E., Kargar, M., Srivastava, D., Szlichta, J.: A variational neural architecture for skill-based team formation. ACM Trans. Inf. Syst. (2023)
14. Kay, M., Matuszek, C., Munson, S.A.: Unequal representation and gender stereotypes in image search results for occupations. In: Proceedings of the 33rd Annual ACM Conference on Human Factors in Computing Systems (2015)
15. Kullback, S., Leibler, R.A.: On information and sufficiency. Ann. Math. Stat. (1951)
16. Loghmani, H., Fani, H.: Bootless application of greedy re-ranking algorithms in fair neural team formation. In: Boratto, L., Faralli, S., Marras, M., Stilo, G. (eds.) Advances in Bias and Fairness in Information Retrieval (2023)
17. Pitoura, E., Stefanidis, K., Koutrika, G.: Fairness in rankings and recommendations: an overview. VLDB J. (2022)
18. Rad, R.H., Bagheri, E., Kargar, M., Srivastava, D., Szlichta, J.: Subgraph representation learning for team mining. In: WebSci (2022)
19. Rad, R.H., Fani, H., Kargar, M., Szlichta, J., Bagheri, E.: Learning to form skill-based teams of experts. In: CIKM 2020 (2020)
20. Sapienza, A., Goyal, P., Ferrara, E.: Deep neural networks for optimal team composition. Front. Big Data (2019)
21. Zehlike, M., Castillo, C.: Reducing disparate exposure in ranking: a learning to rank approach. In: Proceedings of The Web Conference 2020, WWW 2020. Association for Computing Machinery, New York, NY, USA (2020)

Simultaneous Unlearning of Multiple Protected User Attributes From Variational Autoencoder Recommenders Using Adversarial Training

Gustavo Escobedo[1](✉)[iD], Christian Ganhör[1][iD], Stefan Brandl[1][iD], Mirjam Augstein[3][iD], and Markus Schedl[1,2][iD]

[1] Johannes Kepler University Linz, Linz, Austria
{gustavo.escobedo,christian.ganhoer,stefan.brandl,markus.schedl}@jku.at
[2] Linz Institute of Technology, Linz, Austria
[3] University of Applied Sciences Upper Austria, Hagenberg, Austria
mirjam.augstein@fh-hagenberg.at

Abstract. In widely used neural network-based collaborative filtering models, users' history logs are encoded into latent embeddings that represent the users' preferences. In this setting, the models are capable of mapping users' protected attributes (e.g., gender or ethnicity) from these user embeddings even without explicit access to them, resulting in models that may treat specific demographic user groups unfairly and raise privacy issues. While prior work has approached the removal of a single protected attribute of a user at a time, multiple attributes might come into play in real-world scenarios. In the work at hand, we present AdvXMultVAE which aims to unlearn multiple protected attributes (exemplified by gender and age) simultaneously to improve fairness across demographic user groups. For this purpose, we couple a variational autoencoder (VAE) architecture with adversarial training (AdvMultVAE) to support simultaneous removal of the users' protected attributes with continuous and/or categorical values. Our experiments on two datasets, LFM-2b-100k and ML-1m, from the music and movie domains, respectively, show that our approach can yield better results than its singular removal counterparts (based on AdvMultVAE) in effectively mitigating demographic biases whilst improving the anonymity of latent embeddings.

Keywords: Recommender Systems · Collaborative Filtering · Variational Autoencoder · Privacy · Debiasing

1 Introduction

Recommender system models commonly leverage collaborative information in order to predict the likelihood of an item to be consumed by a user. Most neural network-based recommender models, including MultVAE [10], encode the users' consumption histories into latent vector representations which are used to produce recommendations. Though these latent vectors are based only on user consumption data, they can implicitly encode undesirable biases and sensitive user attributes, which are a potential source of unfairness and privacy issues, respectively [14,16]. As a result, users from specific demographic groups may be treated unfairly regarding the quality and/or diversity of recommendations. Furthermore, users' protected information (e.g., gender, ethnicity, age) is subject to potential exposure through adversarial attacks [3], which directly harms the trustworthiness of recommender models [17].

To tackle these issues, prior work [4] applied adversarial information removal techniques in order to remove the users' gender information from latent vectors while maintaining similar recommendation performance. However, in real-world scenarios, additional protected attributes such as age or country might be encoded in latent space at the same time. Therefore, in this work, we introduce AdvXMultVAE that aims at jointly removing several protected attributes by extending the AdvMultVAE architecture [4] to support simultaneous removal of user-protected attributes (continuous and/or categorical). For our experiments, we leverage two publicly available datasets that include protected attributes: a subset of LFM-2b[1], which we name LFM-2b-100k, and ML-1m[2] from the music and movie domains, respectively. We evaluate the proposed AdvXMultVAE against AdvMultVAE by studying the removal of gender (categorical) and age (continuous) attributes under different degrees of removal aggressiveness. Our results indicate that AdvXMultVAE can outperform or are on-par with the baselines in terms of gender and age removal while maintaining competing performance in terms of NDCG and Recall.

2 Related Work

Adversarial training techniques have been used for removing protected user attribute information from latent embeddings to learn fair and privacy-preserving representations in classification and retrieval tasks [1,6,8,18]. Also recommendation models are not exempt of privacy-related threats [3]. Therefore, prior work introduced several mitigation approaches. For instance, Wang et al. [19] presented a VAE-based disentangled encoder and an attacker network to avoid membership inference attacks by removing biases from training data. Furthermore, Liu et al. [11] applied removal of gender to mitigate user data exposure and improve fairness in GNN-based recommenders. Also, Li et al. [9] proposed an adversarial learning approach to generate filters for user embeddings to remove different combinations of categorical user protected attributes to improve fairness in matrix-factorization based recommenders. In addition, Ganhör et al. [4] introduced AdvMultVAE in order to unlearn users' gender information from latent embeddings while maintaining recommendation accuracy. In this work, we also focus on learning privacy-preserving representations in VAE

---
[1] http://www.cp.jku.at/datasets/LFM-2b/.
[2] https://grouplens.org/datasets/movielens/1m/.

recommenders, but different from previous approaches where users' protected attributes are treated one at a time, we perform simultaneous attribute removal.

3 Method

We briefly introduce the MultVAE and AdvMultVAE models and their components followed by the description of our proposed AdvXMultVAE architecture.

The MultVAE [10] is a recommendation model that consists of two sub-networks, namely, an encoder $f(\cdot)$ and a decoder $g(\cdot)$. The encoder transforms the users' implicit preferences vector x into the latent distribution $\mathcal{N}(\mu, \sigma)$ characterized by the learnable parameters μ and σ using a Gaussian prior $\mathcal{N}(0, I)$ from which the latent vector z is sampled. The vector z serves as input to the decoder sub-network $g(\cdot)$, generating $g(z)$ which is used to reconstruct the original users' implicit preferences vector x through the minimization of the reconstruction loss $\mathcal{L}^{REC}(g(z), x)$ and the regularization term $\mathcal{L}^{KL}(\mathcal{N}(\mu, \sigma), \mathcal{N}(0, I))$, defined as the Kullback-Leibler divergence between the estimated latent distribution given by the parameters μ and σ and its prior. The resultant loss $\mathcal{L}^{MULT}$ is shown in Eq. 1 where the hyperparameter β is introduced as a factor to adjust of regularization power of $\mathcal{L}^{KL}$ which steers the learning to its prior.

$$\mathcal{L}^{MULT} = \mathcal{L}^{REC}(g(z), x) - \beta \mathcal{L}^{KL}(\mathcal{N}(\mu, \sigma), \mathcal{N}(0, I)) \quad (1)$$

The AdvMultVAE [4] model is an extension of MultVAE and is composed of two training phases: an adversarial training phase to remove sensitive information from the latent vectors and an adversarial attack phase aiming to recover remaining information. For the adversarial training, an adversarial network module $h(\cdot)$ is added as an extra prediction head plugged into the output of the encoder $f(\cdot)$. Its main task is to predict the users' protected attribute y from the latent vector z while maintaining recommendation performance. Consequently, the learning process can be defined as a min-max problem where $\mathcal{L}^{MULT}$ is maximized and the adversarial loss $\mathcal{L}^{adv}$ of the adversarial module $h(\cdot)$ is minimized as in Eq. 2.

$$\arg\max_{f,g} \arg\min_{h} \mathcal{L}^{MULT}(x) - \mathcal{L}^{adv}(x, y) \quad (2)$$

In order to make the adversarial training possible through a simple backpropagation process, a gradient reversal layer $grl(\cdot)$ [5] is added to the adversarial module. The purpose of $grl(\cdot)$ is to scale and change the direction of the calculated gradients using a gradient reversal scaling factor λ in the backward pass during training, and work as the identity function during the forward pass. This addition also allows the reformulation of the learning objective, as shown in Eq. 3.

$$\arg\min_{f,g,h} \mathcal{L}^{MULT}(x) + \mathcal{L}^{adv}(x, y) \quad (3)$$

The attack phase of the AdvMultVAE starts after the optimization of the previously introduced learning objective (Eq. 3). In this phase, the resultant trained model, with frozen parameters, is used to train a standalone attacker network

$h^{atk}(\cdot)$ aiming to decipher the remaining sensitive information encoded in the latent vector z generated by the encoder $f(\cdot)$.

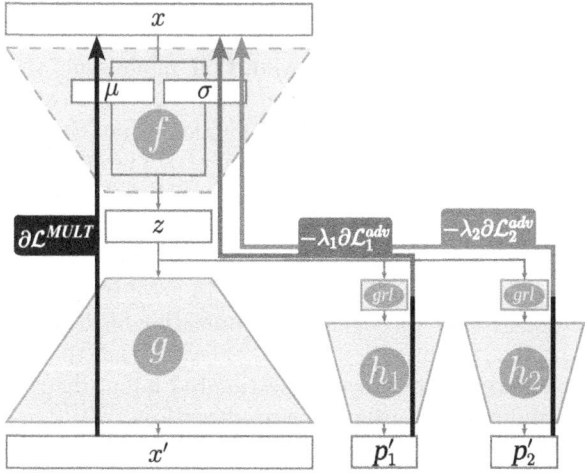

Fig. 1. Outline of our AdvXMultVAE approach. The thin gray arrows flowing from the top to the bottom indicate the forward pass, the bold arrows the backward pass. Here, the red and orange arrows highlight the reversed gradients of the attributes, p_1 and p_2, respectively, that the model should unlearn. (Color figure online)

The architecture of our proposed AdvXMultVAE approach for simultaneous removal of attributes is illustrated in Fig. 1. Formally, we first define the set $\mathcal{P} : \{p_0, p_1, \ldots, p_k\}$ representing the users' k protected attributes, where each p_i, $i \in \{0, \ldots, k\}$, can be of a continuous or categorical type. To unlearn each of these attributes, instead of the single adversarial module in AdvMultVAE, we define a set of corresponding adversarial modules $\mathcal{H} : \{h_0, \ldots, h_k\}$. Each of the modules receives z as input and aims at predicting the protected attribute p_k. Therefore, we define the loss of each module as $\mathcal{L}_k^{adv}(h_k(z), p_k)$ and use cross-entropy (CE) for categorical attributes and mean-squared-error (MSE) for continuous attributes. Given these definitions, we introduce the multi-attribute adversarial loss $\mathcal{L}^{advX}$ (Eq. 4) as the sum of each of the losses assigned to each adversarial module h_k, and integrate it into the final loss, shown in Eq. 5.

$$\mathcal{L}^{advX} = \sum_{k}^{|\mathcal{P}|} \mathcal{L}_k^{adv}(h_k(z), p_k) \qquad (4)$$

$$\arg\min_{f,g,\{h_0,\ldots,h_k\}} \mathcal{L}^{MULT}(x) + \mathcal{L}^{advX}(x, \mathcal{P}) \qquad (5)$$

With this formulation, we are also able to reproduce the previously introduced models by setting adequate values of λs for each module.

Table 1. Statistical description of datasets

Dataset	Users		Items	Interactions	Density
ML-1M	Total	6,040	3,416	999,611	0.0484
	Gender (Male/Female)	4,331/1,709			
	Age (Mean/Std/Median)	30.6/12.9/25.0			
LFM-2B-100K	Total	8,663	47,383	1,476,788	0.0036
	Gender (Male/Female)	7,012/1,651			
	Age (Mean/Std/Median)	25.4/8.4/23.0			

4 Experimental Setup

Datasets. We derived LFM-2B-100K from LFM-2B by only considering users for which we have gender and age information. We then subsample 100k tracks uniformly at random and reinforce 10-core filtering. For ML-1M we adopt 5-core filtering. Table 1 describes the resultant datasets. Furthermore, the users' age information was normalized by scaling the original values in the range [0 : 60] for ML-1M and [0 : 120] for LFM-2B-100K to cover their all their possible values. The resultant dataset is randomly split in 5-folds across users. For each fold, we randomly select 20% of users as test slice, then, the 20% of the remaining users are selected for validation, and the rest for training. We mitigate the imbalanced gender distribution by adding proportional weights to the CE loss of the corresponding adversarial module.

Evaluation. We adopt the *normalized discounted cumulative gain* (NDCG) [7] and Recall metrics to asses the accuracy of recommendation performance for the top 10 recommended items. In addition, we measure the attacker networks' ability to predict protected attributes and we report the corresponding *balanced accuracy* ($BAcc$) [2] for categorical attributes, which values $\sim \frac{1}{\#categories}$ indicate total debiasing of the predicted attribute, therefore, the inability of the attacker network to successfully predict the given attribute (e.g., $BAcc = 0.5$ for binary classification). Moreover, we report the *mean absolute error* (MAE) for continuous attributes, which higher values indicate a stronger debiasing effect achieved.

We report the average and standard deviation for the test slices across 5-folds. In addition, we concatenate the users' individual scores in all folds and then perform Wilcoxon signed-rank tests [15] to asses the statistical significance differences between recommendation models, McNemar's tests [13] to measure the agreement of results of gender attacker networks, and t-tests between age attacker networks' results. All statistical tests are performed with 95% of confidence between the results of different (λ_{Gender}, λ_{Age}) combinations.

Models and Training Procedure. We train our models inspired by the protocol presented in [4]. Consequently, for each dataset, we target the single and simultaneous removal of *age* (continuous) and *gender* (categorical). We fix the following parameters to establish fair conditions of comparison between models: We train all models for 200 epochs for the adversarial removal phase and 50 epochs for the attack phase for both datasets using an Adam optimizer. The adversarial and attacker networks have the same architecture represented by a multi-layer perceptron with one intermediate layer, and according to the type of attribute, one single value for a continuous attribute or a one-hot encoded vector for a categorical attribute is predicted. For the attacking phase, we avoid the sampling step used during the training of the MULTVAE and use the direct output of the encoder $f(\cdot)$ for each user. For each model, we perform an exhaustive grid search to identify optimized combinations of gradient reversal scaling factors λ_{Gender}(gender) and λ_{Age}(age), to observe the effect on performance and debiasing for different degrees of removal aggressiveness. We investigate λ values[3] in [0, 1, 200, 400, 600, 800] due to the difference in magnitude between $\mathcal{L}^{MULT}$ and $\mathcal{L}^{advX}$ that we devised in early experiments. We report results for the best debiasing results of each attribute and present an analysis of all 36 different (λ_{Gender}, λ_{Age}) combinations. The training of the attacker networks is performed regardless of the values of λ_{Gender} and λ_{Age}. The source code of and complete configuration of our experiments can be found in our repository.[4]

Table 2. Experimental results expressed in percentages on the two datasets ML-1M and LFM-2B-100K. The scores in **bold** indicate the best scores across all models. The superscript ♠ indicates statistical significance difference with $p \leq 0.05$ between ADVMULTVAE and ADVXMULTVAE for the given attribute in the suffix of the models' names. The superscript ⋆ indicates statistical significance difference with $p \leq 0.05$ across all models.

Dataset	Model-Attribute	Performance		Debiasing	
		$NDCG \uparrow$	$Recall \uparrow$	$BAcc_G \downarrow$	$MAE_A \uparrow$
ML-1M	MULTVAE	**$62.72_{0.98}^{\star}$**	**$08.16_{0.09}$**	$69.81_{1.82}$	$14.45_{0.38}$
	ADVMULTVAE-G	$61.15_{1.22}$	$07.84_{0.13}$	$59.05_{5.57}$	$14.52_{0.47}$
	ADVXMULTVAE-G	$61.21_{1.11}$	$07.88_{0.10}$	**$57.14_{5.72}^{♠\star}$**	$16.91_{0.39}$
	ADVMULTVAE-A	$62.51_{1.05}^{♠}$	$08.12_{0.04}^{♠}$	$69.33_{1.58}$	**$17.10_{0.42}$**
	ADVXMULTVAE-A	$61.05_{1.16}$	$07.86_{0.10}$	$59.02_{3.82}$	$17.09_{0.43}$
LFM-2B-100K	MULTVAE	$47.46_{0.24}$	$06.54_{0.22}$	$67.00_{1.43}$	$04.28_{0.16}$
	ADVMULTVAE-G	$46.52_{0.23}^{♠}$	$06.41_{0.12}^{♠}$	$53.03_{2.51}$	$04.32_{0.18}$
	ADVXMULTVAE-G	$45.88_{0.29}$	$06.27_{0.16}$	**$52.81_{1.79}^{♠\star}$**	$04.33_{0.16}$
	ADVMULTVAE-A	$47.42_{0.34}^{♠}$	**$06.59_{0.12}^{♠}$**	$68.02_{1.38}$	$04.37_{0.13}$
	ADVXMULTVAE-A	$46.77_{0.28}$	$06.45_{0.17}$	$53.37_{1.63}$	**$04.40_{0.16}^{♠\star}$**

---

[3] We include $\lambda = 1$ for maximal removal as in the original formulation [5].
[4] https://github.com/hcai-mms/advx-multvae.

5 Results and Analyses

In this Section, we first analyze the overall performance of the investigated models and then we present a analysis on the multiple debiasing objective and the impact of different (λ_{Gender}, λ_{Age}) combinations on debiasing and recommendation performance for the ML-1M dataset.

5.1 Overall Performance

Table 2 shows the performance of various models and attacker networks. We split the results in three groups according to the explored attribute, identified by the suffixes G (gender) and A (age). Each row represents the best debiasing results in percentages for the attribute in the suffix of each model's name. Each score's subscript indicate the standard deviation across 5-folds.

In the Table 2, the removal of gender (AdvMultVAE-G and AdvXMultVAE-G) for both datasets has similar improvements in terms of $BAcc_G$. However, when targeting the removal of age (AdvMultVAE-A and AdvXMultVAE-A), we obtain a substantial improvement in terms of MAE_A for the ML-1M dataset and are very similar MAE_A values for the LFM-2B-100K dataset, which might reflect the differences of user's age values distributions between the two studied datasets, and also a lower correlation between users preferences and their declared age in the LastFM platform which we take a limitation for this work.

For AdvMultVAE, we observe that targeting gender removal causes a ~3% drop in NDCG and Recall for both datasets, as expected [4], compared to MultVAE showing a substantial drop in $BAcc_G$ of ~15–20%. The age removal, leads to a ~17% increase of MAE_A for ML-1M and remains the same for LFM-2B-100K. Also, AdvMultVAE-A and AdvMultVAE-G's results show that the single removal of gender has a slight indirect effect on the removal of age and vice-versa. We speculate that the difference in the removal effect might be due to the difference in magnitude of the gradients that the MSE an CE adversarial networks objective yield.

Our approach AdvXMultVAE obtains similar NDCG values and shows the best mean values of $BAcc_G$ with a slight difference in MAE_A for both datasets in comparison to AdvMultVAE and presents an overlap if we examine their standard deviation values (e.g., $BAcc_G$ values for AdvMultVAE-G and AdvXMultVAE-G). Nonetheless, except for $BAcc_G$ of AdvXMultVAE-G, all the best reported debiasing metrics are statistically significant. Furthermore, AdvXMultVAE's results indicate a trade-off between $BAcc_G$ and MAE_A, when we target the best removal of each attribute on both datasets. However, this trade-off does not have a great impact across all examined metrics.

5.2 Multiple Debiasing Objective Behavior

To delve into the behavior all the explored (λ_{Gender}, λ_{Age}) combinations and the multiple debiasing objective behavior, Fig. 2 shows all values of debiasing metrics for the ML-1M dataset with their corresponding NDCG scores for all (λ_{Gender}, λ_{Age}) pairs. Each point of the distribution represents one (λ_{Gender}, λ_{Age}) combination and the different models are represented by different shapes. We also include dotted lines which represent the debiasing scores obtained for MULTVAE as reference for the analysis.

The distribution of points in Fig. 2 illustrates the trade-off between debiasing power and recommendation performance, where the models in the upper-left region have stronger debiasing capabilities and higher NDCG values in the lower-right corner. Moreover, the variants to the right of the vertical dotted line indicate higher $BAcc_G$ values than MULTVAE but obtain similar NDCG values (we explore this effect in more detail in Subsect. 5.3). Furthermore, the ADVMULTVAE variants are in the vicinity of the dotted lines which indicates a mild influence on the debiasing of one attribute onto the other, this also can be observed in Table 2.

Our approach ADVXMULTVAE can achieve stronger debiasing capabilities than their ADVMULTVAE counterparts with a marginal drop in recommendation performance for both attributes, and especially for gender. This is indicated by the presence of ADVXMULTVAE points on the upper-left corner and towards the direction of our multiple debiasing objective. Also, the corresponding performance values in this region are not drastically lower than those of the ADVMULTVAE and MULTVAE variants. Additionally, some ADVXMULTVAE removal variants on the upper-left corner show slightly better NDCG than those in the upper-middle region, which indicates that more aggressive simultaneous removal can yield higher accuracy in some cases. We observe that it is possible to realize age removal to a substantial extent with only a marginal drop in NDCG, which is indicated by the removal variants in the upper-right corner. Furthermore some ADVXMULTVAE variants lay close to the dotted lines and correspond to the configurations when λ_{Gender} or λ_{Age} is set to 1 which results in similar behavior to the ADVMULTVAE variants.

In order to show the ability of the attacker networks to map real the distribution of the users' gender, we show t-SNE [12] plots of the first and second dimensions of the user's latent embeddings of our three variants for the ML-1M dataset in the Fig. 3. Alongside each plot's axes, we show the corresponding density of the distributions of predicted gender. Figure 3a shows a distribution of the two predicted classes for the ADVMULTVAE model where the densities of the two classes are visibly discordant. In contrast, we observe that the distributions are less discordant for the ADVMULTVAE (Fig. 3b) and ADVXMULTVAE (Fig. 3c) variants which indicates that is harder to infer gender information after applying adversarial removal. Additionally, our approach ADVXMULTVAE (Fig. 3c), shows the most overlap between distributions of gender, therefore, yields the most privacy-preserving user's latent embeddings.

5.3 Interaction of Multiple Gradient Reversal Scaling Factors

In order to observe the interaction of the explored values of lambdas, Fig. 4 shows how these values affect debiasing and recommendation performance for the ML-1M dataset. We set the λ_{Gender} values in the x-axis and the average across

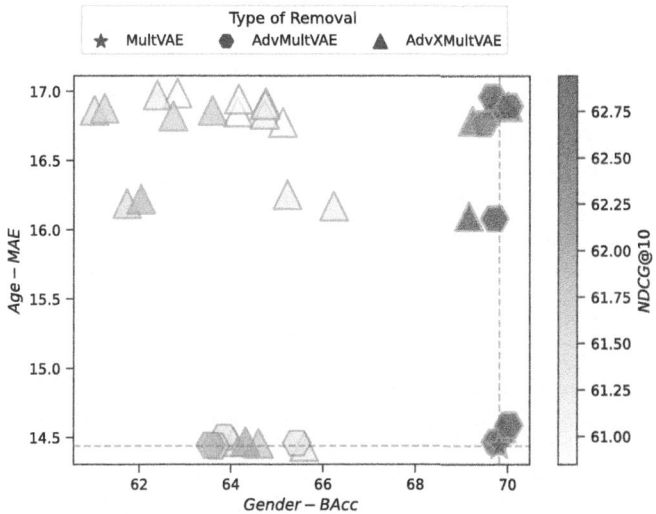

Fig. 2. Performance for debiasing ($BAcc_G$ and MAE_A) and recommendation accuracy ($NDCG@10$) for the ML-1M dataset. Points on the upper-left corner refer to the best privacy-preserving models where the AdvXMultVAE removal variants yield the strongest debiasing power with a marginal loss in terms of NDCG. The intersection of the dotted lines represent the model without debiasing (MultVAE).

5-folds of NDCG (*left*), $BAcc_G$ (*middle*), and MAE_A (*right*) as the y-axis for each subplot respectively. Each subplot shows different lines corresponding to the studied λ_{Age} values. The dotted lines represent the scores for MultVAE as a reference for the analysis.

In the *left* subplot, we observe a consistent decrease of the NDCG values when we increase the both values of lambda. More specifically, when only gender is removed ($\lambda_{Age}= 0$) we obtain higher NDCG values across the different λ_{Gender} values, which indicates the trade-off of performance and debiasing of more than one attribute. Also, when $\lambda_{Gender}\sim 1$, we can even achieve slightly higher NDCG than MultVAE's for $\lambda_{Age}= 200$.

In the *middle* subplot, a pronounced $BAcc_G$ drop when $\lambda_{Gender}\geq 200$ for all the λ_{Age} values, and especially for $\lambda_{Age}= 600$ and $\lambda_{Age}= 200$ where we can see the positive effect of simultaneously removing both attributes. Moreover, we observe a negative impact to the debiasing of gender presenting an increasing tendency of $BAcc_G$ values when $\lambda_{Gender}\geq 600$. Also, the best removal of gender is observed when $\lambda_{Gender}= 400$ and $\lambda_{Age}= 400$. Moreover, when $\lambda_{Gender}\sim 1$, we can even achieve slightly worse $BAcc_G$ than MultVAE's results, which was also observed in Fig. 2.

In the *right* subplot, the values of MAE_A present slight fluctuations across the different values of λ_{Gender}, and a more pronounced debiasing effect when $\lambda_{Age}\geq 200$. Moreover, when $\lambda_{Age}\geq 400$, we obtain similar MAE_A values, which

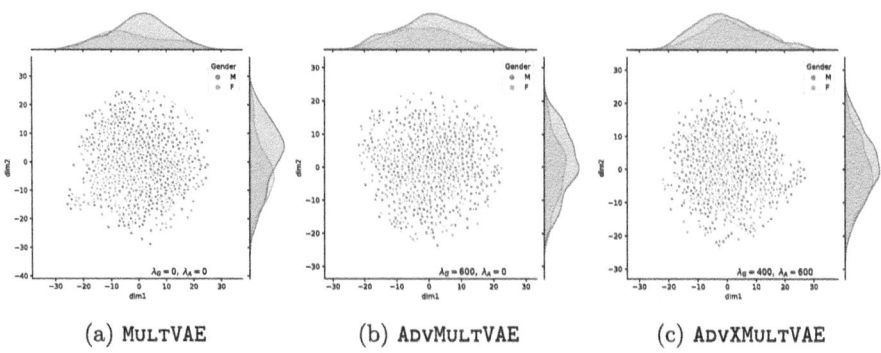

Fig. 3. t-SNE plots of the users' latent embeddings and attacker networks' predictions of gender for the ML-1M dataset, each plot includes the density of the distribution for each gender across the corresponding latent dimension.

might indicate a removal saturation point for λ_{Age}. Furthermore, the best MAE_A value is achieved when $\lambda_{Gender}= 600$ and $\lambda_{Age}= 600$.

Overall, from Fig. 4, we can establish that using high values of λ_{Age} and λ_{Gender} leads to a consistent drop of NDCG. Additionally, using high values of λ_{Gender} has a detrimental effect on the debiasing of gender which we speculate to be an effect of steering the encoder updates to the objective of the adversarial modules during training. Also, the multiple λ_{Gender} explored values do not influence the removal of age which might indicate low dependency between these two private attributes.

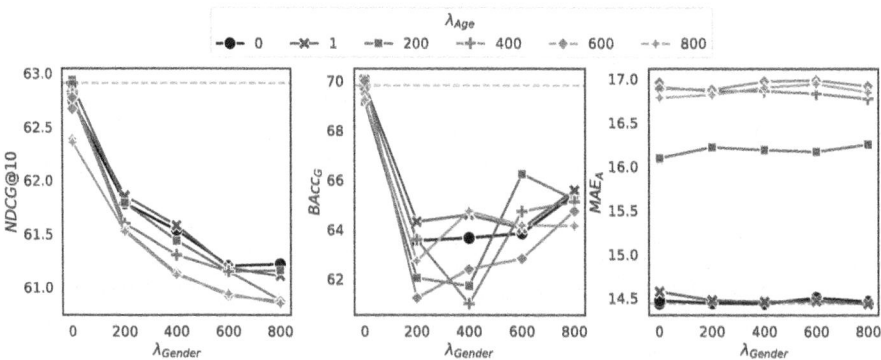

Fig. 4. Interaction of different gradient scaling factors (λ_{Gender}, λ_{Age}) and reported metrics for the ML-1M dataset. Each subplot indicates the obtained mean values of NDCG, $BAcc_G$, and MAE_A respectively from left to right.

6 Conclusion

In this work, we presented ADVXMULTVAE to address the simultaneous removal of users' multiple protected attributes of continuous and categorical types, using adversarial training in a variational autoencoder architecture. Our results show that the simultaneous removal of gender and age can yield stronger debiasing capabilities to its single-attribute removal counterparts with a slight drop in recommendation performance. Further work could explore the debiasing of more than two attributes, for which our architecture can easily be extended, as well as experimenting with other attributes, e.g. personality traits. Also, the simultaneous removal of attributes could be applied to other representations, such as item embeddings (to unlearn music artist's gender information, for instance), as well as recommendation algorithms beyond VAEs.

Acknowledgments. This research was funded in whole or in part by the Austrian Science Fund (FWF): P36413, P33526, and DFH-23, and by the State of Upper Austria and the Federal Ministry of Education, Science, and Research, through grants LIT-2021-YOU-215 and LIT-2020-9-SEE-113.

Disclosure of Interests. The authors have no competing interests to declare that are relevant to the content of this article.

References

1. Beigi, G., Liu, H.: A survey on privacy in social media: identification, mitigation, and applications. ACM/IMS Trans. Data Sci. **1**(1) (2020). https://doi.org/10.1145/3343038
2. Brodersen, K.H., Ong, C.S., Stephan, K.E., Buhmann, J.M.: The balanced accuracy and its posterior distribution. In: 20th International Conference on Pattern Recognition, ICPR 2010, Istanbul, Turkey, 23–26 August 2010, pp. 3121–3124. IEEE Computer Society (2010). https://doi.org/10.1109/ICPR.2010.764
3. Deldjoo, Y., Noia, T.D., Merra, F.A.: A survey on adversarial recommender systems: from attack/defense strategies to generative adversarial networks. ACM Comput. Surv. **54**(2), 35:1–35:38 (2022). https://doi.org/10.1145/3439729
4. Ganhör, C., Penz, D., Rekabsaz, N., Lesota, O., Schedl, M.: Unlearning protected user attributes in recommendations with adversarial training. In: Proceedings of the 45th International ACM SIGIR Conference on Research and Development in Information Retrieval, SIGIR 2022, pp. 2142–2147. Association for Computing Machinery, New York, NY, USA (2022). https://doi.org/10.1145/3477495.3531820
5. Ganin, Y., Lempitsky, V.: Unsupervised domain adaptation by backpropagation. In: Bach, F., Blei, D. (eds.) Proceedings of the 32nd International Conference on Machine Learning. Proceedings of Machine Learning Research, vol. 37, pp. 1180–1189. PMLR, Lille, France, 07–09 July 2015. https://proceedings.mlr.press/v37/ganin15.html
6. Hauzenberger, L., Masoudian, S., Kumar, D., Schedl, M., Rekabsaz, N.: Modular and on-demand bias mitigation with attribute-removal subnetworks. In: Findings of the Association for Computational Linguistics: ACL 2023, pp. 6192–6214. Association for Computational Linguistics, Toronto, Canada, July 2023. https://doi.org/10.18653/v1/2023.findings-acl.386

7. Järvelin, K., Kekäläinen, J.: Cumulated gain-based evaluation of IR techniques. ACM Trans. Inf. Syst. **20**(4), 422–446 (2002). https://doi.org/10.1145/582415.582418
8. Kumar, D., et al.: Parameter-efficient modularised bias mitigation via Adapter-Fusion. In: Proceedings of the 17th Conference of the European Chapter of the Association for Computational Linguistics, pp. 2738–2751. Association for Computational Linguistics, Dubrovnik, Croatia, May 2023. https://doi.org/10.18653/v1/2023.eacl-main.201. https://aclanthology.org/2023.eacl-main.201
9. Li, Y., Chen, H., Xu, S., Ge, Y., Zhang, Y.: Towards personalized fairness based on causal notion. In: Proceedings of the 44th International ACM SIGIR Conference on Research and Development in Information Retrieva, SIGIR 2021. Association for Computing Machinery, New York, NY, USA (2021). https://doi.org/10.1145/3404835.3462966
10. Liang, D., Krishnan, R.G., Hoffman, M.D., Jebara, T.: Variational autoencoders for collaborative filtering. In: Proceedings of the 2018 World Wide Web Conference, WWW 2018, pp. 689–698. International World Wide Web Conferences Steering Committee, Republic and Canton of Geneva, CHE (2018). https://doi.org/10.1145/3178876.3186150
11. Liu, H., Wang, Y., Lin, H., Xu, B., Zhao, N.: Mitigating sensitive data exposure with adversarial learning for fairness recommendation systems. Neural Comput. Appl. **34**(20), 18097–18111 (2022). https://doi.org/10.1007/s00521-022-07373-4
12. Van der Maaten, L., Hinton, G.: Visualizing data using t-SNE. J. Mach. Learn. Res. **9**(11) (2008)
13. McNemar, Q.: Note on the sampling error of the difference between correlated proportions or percentages. Psychometrika **12**(2), 153–157 (1947)
14. Melchiorre, A.B., Rekabsaz, N., Parada-Cabaleiro, E., Brandl, S., Lesota, O., Schedl, M.: Investigating gender fairness of recommendation algorithms in the music domain. Inf. Process. Manag. **58**(5), 102666 (2021). https://doi.org/10.1016/j.ipm.2021.102666. https://www.sciencedirect.com/science/article/pii/S0306457321001540
15. Rey, D., Neuhäuser, M.: Wilcoxon-Signed-Rank Test, pp. 1658–1659. Springer, Heidelberg (2011). https://doi.org/10.1007/978-3-642-04898-2_616
16. Schedl, M., Rekabsaz, N., Lex, E., Grosz, T., Greif, E.: Multiperspective and multidisciplinary treatment of fairness in recommender systems research. In: Adjunct Proceedings of the 30th ACM Conference on User Modeling, Adaptation and Personalization, UMAP 2022 Adjunct, pp. 90–94. Association for Computing Machinery, New York, NY, USA (2022). https://doi.org/10.1145/3511047.3536400
17. Wang, S., Zhang, X., Wang, Y., Ricci, F.: Trustworthy recommender systems. ACM Trans. Intell. Syst. Technol. (2023). https://doi.org/10.1145/3627826. Just Accepted
18. Wang, Y., Ma, W., Zhang, M., Liu, Y., Ma, S.: A survey on the fairness of recommender systems. ACM Trans. Inf. Syst. **41**(3) (2023). https://doi.org/10.1145/3547333
19. Wang, Z., et al.: Debiasing learning for membership inference attacks against recommender systems. In: Proceedings of the 28th ACM SIGKDD Conference on Knowledge Discovery and Data Mining, KDD 2022, pp. 1959–1968. Association for Computing Machinery, New York, NY, USA (2022). https://doi.org/10.1145/3534678.3539392

Author Index

A
Augstein, Mirjam 91

B
Bartley, Nathan 64
Boaye Belle, Alvine 46
Brandl, Stefan 91
Burghardt, Keith 64

C
Caverlee, James 32

E
Escobedo, Gustavo 91

F
Fani, Hossein 78

G
Ganhör, Christian 91

H
Hemmati, Hadi 46

J
Jiang, Zhen Ming (Jack) 46

L
Lerman, Kristina 64
Loghmani, Hamed 78

M
Ma, Shichao 16
Moasses, Roonak 78
Mohajer, Mohammad Mahdi 46

O
Onishi, Takeshi 32

R
Rajaei, Delaram 78
Rystrøm, Jonathan H. 1

S
Saeedi, Mahdis 78
Schedl, Markus 91
Shiri Harzevili, Nima 46

W
Wang, Junjie 46
Wang, Song 46

SPRINGER NATURE

GPSR Compliance

The European Union's (EU) General Product Safety Regulation (GPSR) is a set of rules that requires consumer products to be safe and our obligations to ensure this.

If you have any concerns about our products, you can contact us on ProductSafety@springernature.com

In case Publisher is established outside the EU, the EU authorized representative is:

Springer Nature Customer Service Center GmbH
Europaplatz 3
69115 Heidelberg, Germany

The manufacturer's authorised representative in the EU is Springer Nature Customer Service Centre GmbH, Europaplatz 3, 69115 Heidelberg, Germany. If you have any concerns regarding our products, please contact ProductSafety@springernature.com

Printed and bound by CPI Group (UK) Ltd, Croydon, CR0 4YY

25/03/2026

02078197-0012